A Way To Home:
New and Selected Poems

Martin Galvin

Other Books By the Author

Sounding the Atlantic
Circling Out
Appetites (out of print)
Making Beds (out of print)
Wild Card

Reviews of Martin Galvin's Poetry

About **Wild Card**, 1989:

"He's the only one who knows how to write a line."

> –Howard Nemerov, judge, distinguished poet and Poet Laureate of the United States, 1989. *The Washington Post*, 1989 in selecting *Wild Card* for The Poetry Committee of the Greater Washington D.C. Area 1989 Book Award.

"Martin Galvin's book takes a…more sardonic look at our times populating his poems with people who have somehow let life pass them by…cocktail loungers who are 'Picassoesque grotesques'…Galvin presents these lost souls and others with wit, compassion and intelligence. This is a book of the all too familiar, 'the ceremony of the world coming together.' But what escape is there? For one, there's the imagination, as when the poet's daughter suddenly breaks through the dreary absurdities by announcing 'The moon is like a door knob.' Secondly, there's the natural world…Galvin offers an exceptionally lovely lyric on life's inherent possibilities. By balancing fierce irony and keen wit with this sort of gentle and lovely testament, Galvin has produced a very fine first collection of poems."

> –Paul Genega, *Washington Review*, October/November 1990.

"Indeed, his work bounces from the elegiac to the perverse, and, more often fuses the two. He is part Flannery O'Connor, part W. H. Auden and in all an observer and filter of random events."

> –Tracey O' Shaughnessy, author, journalist, the *Republlican-American*, Waterbury, CT

"…I absolutely love (OK I'm shouting!) 'Weathering the Front Door.' At the end I felt as if I were dancing. I love the colloquial way you talk. What a great way to de-scribe 'the bride and groom reel/from the garden path into the house and bed.' …and then that final line. I'm going to go back to it when I need a pick-me-up."

> –Barri Armitage, poet and musician, author of *Double Helix*

About **Sounding the Atlantic**, *2010:*

"It's a real treasure trove, with poems born of every kind of mood and narrators who range from a 15 year old 'Valley Girl' kiss collector to a one-eyed, middle-aged hillbilly skunk hater. There's much in the way of wisdom and insight, precise observation and dazzling metaphoric connectedness, and, best of all, there are turns and turnabouts of language that are like the acrobatics of your trapeze artist.... *Sounding the Atlantic* is truly a signal achievement. Out of thin air...you've cooked up a feast of pleasures for anyone who can read."

    –Kermit Moyer, author of *The Chester Chronicles*

"It has been an absolute delight to amble through your new book. The people you create, the stories you tell, are quite wonderful. I certainly haven't finished picking it up, getting lost in the words, assimilating, then moving on...each day a new wonder. This one has to be a prize winner and let me be one of the surely many—before the event—to give you a hearty congratulations. Thank you!"

    –Sherry Stanley, poet

"...I dig your lines, taut and snug at both ends, and great rhythms.... I also was intrigued by such attention to voice.... I teach fiction and poetry and your strong narratives and character/voice in poetry would be a good lesson...your 'Passive Aggressive' poem will likely find its way into my creative writing class this semester...."

    –Todd B. Rudy, Cornell University, 2002

About **Circling Out**, 2007:

"In the beautifully wrought book, *Circling Out*, we find Martin Galvin's poems immediately steeped in his Irish Catholic heritage. One is reminded of that country and its legacy as in the work of Seamus Heaney or Evan Boland. We enter a strong sense of place, yet Galvin holds his own in originality, simile, metaphor, language, and idea. Still, it is a comfort and a blessing (as the Irish might say) to hear a voice from the rich landscape of a country with such strong and ancient tradition of poetry, this Celtic land of Atlantic Europe."

    –*Montserrat Review*, Mary Morris, poet

A Way To Home:
New and Selected Poems

Martin Galvin

Paintings by Ryan Bongers

Poets' Choice Publishing

Consultant work:
www.WilliamMeredithFoundation.org

Bulk discounts available through www.Poets-Choice.com

Cover art: Ryan Bongers
"Red Tree," oil on panel
Author's photo by: Theresa Galvin
Art editor: Barbara Shaw

Library of Congress Cataloging-in-Publication Data pending
ISBN 978-0-9972629-2-6

Poets' Choice

Poets' Choice Publishing
337 Kitemaug Road
Uncasville, CT 06382
Poets-Choice.com

For Rod Jellema
whose way with words
brought this book home.

How the Artist Met the Author

It was thirty-some years ago, the very first day of my junior year at Walt Whitman High School. I barged in late on Dr. Martin Galvin's Advanced Placement English class. Because I had not applied in time, my name was not listed; this was just a clumsy, last ditch effort to squeeze myself in.

Dr. Galvin asked me why I wished for advanced placement, and why, particularly, his course. I stammered something about taking the AP test, and that I heard he was a really great teacher.

He shook his head and sighed. This course was not a prerequisite for that test, he said, gravely. And his class was already full. He allowed me use of the single vacant seat, in the back of the room, just for the day.

But I stayed for two more years, dragged that seat to the front row, and was grateful—after each and every lesson with this man who had a twinkle in his eye and a twist in his moustache—that I had the gall to burst into his classroom that day, and he the gumption to keep me.

I was dazzled by Martin Galvin's wit and his ability to juggle the solemn with the absurd. He taught me to love words—how to aim precisely and release them profoundly—and convinced me to read and to write with intent. Later I discovered how these skills in writing were also integral to the craft of living.

After graduating from high school, I travelled for many months in Europe, by train and by thumb, all the while sending Martin hand-written, airmail letters, which were anecdotes gleaned from my journey. I simply wanted him to know I was writing, and that I was thinking and seeing the world differently, thanks to him.

Although we live on opposite sides of an ocean, our contact, our friendship endure and grow, as does the deep admiration I have for this very special man.

I was in awe of Martin Galvin from the back row, that very first day, and have been ever since.

—Ryan Bongers

I dedicate the images in this book to my mother,
my very first teacher, my friend, and fellow painter.

Table of Contents

from **_Sounding the Atlantic_** (2010)

Gallery II: Still Lifes   155

from ***Wild Card*** (1989)

Preface

One of the pleasures of wearing my newly-acquired publishers hat is receiving manuscripts from people I have never met, which is the case for Martin Galvin. But, as Rod Jellema says in his introduction, "The best way to get to know Martin Galvin is through his poetry."

This is a poet and teacher who has become something of a legend in the Washington area, and so it was easy to say yes to the friends and former students who were anxious to have his latest work see the light of day, especially given his recent health challenges. What a real joy it has been to read these wonderful poems and get a sense of the exquisitely compassionate and sensitive mind informing them.

One after another, here are poems with unique insight, remarkably, surprisingly, beautifully expressed. Galvin is incomparable, though one thinks of the music of Richard Wilbur, the wit of Philip Larkin, Phillip Levine's sympathy for the common man, the Irish lilt of Seamus Heaney.

Galvin can write convincingly about anything from the "little bones of sleeping bears growing strong inside the snow," to the single tree falling "to meet the quiet call of gravity." His subjects include war, nature, women, country folk, youth, age, illness, health, Irish boys fighting at Antietam to escape, "a bed as empty as the English heart." His dramatic monolog, "Hilda and Me and Hazel" is an hilarious account of country spinsters with a dark back story that makes one think of Frost's "Vanishing Red" or Browning's "My last Duchess." Poets are sometimes described as shamans, or shape changers for their ability to see things we do not see. Galvin's poem, "Blind Girl" ends this way.

> Describe for me the color of clean.
> I'll tell you how a scrubbing feels inside.
> And when you see the conductor raise his stick,
> I'll tell you how the hidden drums will march
> to wake the sleepy violins

No one has written more intelligently of the artistic process, describing even the hunters of Lescaux who pre-date known human consciousness:

> Her fingers told her it was time
> to empty her head of the strange goings-on
> inside, so she found a cave full of the dark
>
> she fed on for its own sake, a place she loved,
> and seeing another animal inside her eye,
> she picked a handy wall and carved him there.

In another poem dealing with Lescaux, art leads to primordial worship:

> The night wolf is eating the baby light again.
>   The last time that happened, you disobeyed
>   And went alone into the big dark.
> We thought the night wolf's whelp had you
>   In their den. We thought that you had gone
>   Over the breath mountain to a place beyond,
> That your life was chosen to replace the taken.
>
> Now you have chipped at our cave wall
>   And an animal we do not know stares
>   Always onto our food and into our sleep
> As if the night wolf eats again.
>   Go now outside and pray to the Light God
>   That he throw his spears at the night wolf
> So we may be safe in the time before he comes to stay.
>
> Let his deep grumble of a voice scare the wolf away.
>   Pray that he speak soon that we may be forgiven.

A religious sensibility often enters into the work, especially when dealing with the aging process. He forgives even the arrogant Blue Jay with a final prayer:

> Tent caterpillars are not beautiful, as we know,
> They take their meals and treats
> And build their houses in trees we love
> And can ruin them for man and bird alike.
> We shall not deal with why such beasts exist,
> The point to allow is that blue jays have
> Their purposes: and we've heard they die
> Like the rest of us, which solves the pride they are.
> But not too soon, Lord of Infinite Design,
> We pray for them and us, not too soon.

In the very moving, possibly autobiographical poem, "Artisan," shifting sands teach the "stroked man" anew, "How to/put aside what has been done/and find his happiness in absences." The old man in "Beyond the Hot Sun," "lets himself be seen by us for what he is/and shrugs for what he isn't anymore."

In my decades of caring for William Meredith after his stroke, the courage and grace it took to shrug at his fate and continue on with joy in life was perhaps the most re-markable spiritual achievement I witnessed in his life, even overshadowing his talent as a poet. I've yet to meet Marvin Galvin, but he and William seem to be brothers in the art, cut from the same cloth. Galvin addresses a friend in a poem this way: "We are happy to be more than we are, You and I placid, at peace in our pain." Some-times happiness comes simply from "The joy of taking pebbles from one's shoes."

Chief among the friends who have worked with us in producing this book is Martin Galvin's wife Theresa. She co-ordinated the exquisite images found in the galleries from Ryan Bongers, Galvin's long-time friend and former student. (Art Editor, Barbara Shaw has assembled them into the beautiful galleries gracing the manuscript throughout). Theresa created an index of titles and proofed the manuscript, essential "housekeeping" elements of any publication, and I surmise had a hand in helping to select which poems to be included. Like Penelope, faithful wife of Odysseus, she has woven and re-woven the poetic threads of this book into a final triumphant tapestry until the heroic poet has found his way to home. How lucky we are to have shared his journey.

–Richard Harteis

INTRODUCTION:
Martin Galvin: Poems That Are Their Voices

Martin Galvin's work shows us that poems say things just the way most people would say them if only they could.

What first cocks the reader's ear to a Galvin poem could be a light lilting of Irish speech, echoing his boyhood neighborhood in Philadelphia. It's more than that, though. The voice of a Galvin poem, often quirky and edged with humor, is sometimes angular and cleverly hooked; it is almost always intimate and folksy; and yet, O so often, it's a voice that is lyrical and tender. And his own ear for the cadences of human speech gives his poems a plainness and economy that all of us talkers must envy. Listen to his way of catching our fear of the dark woods:

> We name night's trees to hold away what scares us
> As our oldest ancestors did the oldest vengeful gods.
> We call them what we recognize against April's sky:
> Our memories sharpened by fear of crucifixion.
> . . . .
> In the morning. . .
> The scraggled trees are only trees, not ancient aches. . .
> The wind softs down
> From the eastern hills and it is nearly time
> To go to work, to school, to comfort other men
> That what they'd seen last night they hadn't seen
> And that the path we're on is where we mean to go.

Or, again, for slight contrast, here is a voice remembering itself as a teenage boy, the voice sounding a little like Huck Finn's:

> I didn't have a girl to tell things to, what I'd seen,
> So I went out and got one, the standard issue
> Smart-between-the-ears kind, the way girls get
> Way before guys do from our quaint bringing up.

I like to think these are ways the poet inside us would like to speak.

Yet, even so, I see the poet Galvin as a solid refutation of the notion, commonly laid down as a rule in poetry workshops, that *the poet must strive to find his or her own voice.* I think not. An invitation to monotony on the road to boredom. Good poets like Martin Galvin find myriad voices for hundreds of poems. It is a profound fact that we readers hear mad Lear's voice, or more-than-comic Falstaff's, or the deep femininity in Cleopatra's, but we never hear Shakespeare's. Likewise, to a degree, what we hear in Galvin's poems is not limited to "his own" individual voice.

We can easily believe that Galvin has lain prone in the grass when he tells us he

> Got nose to nose with ants, I did,
> To get our signals straight about our needs,

but his lively imagination moves him to speak in many ways. For example, in one poem he speaks *as* a retired salesman of used vacuum cleaners; in others, he speaks *for* an immigrant hired as a chicken-chaser, or *about* a woman who day after day shucks clams. There are wonderful, slightly eccentric and sometimes just lovely poems about birds, a toad, the winter stillness of a place called Heron Bay. The voices saying these poems are tuned to their subjects. Liberated from the monotone sameness of a poet's individual voice, these poems make their own voices. And thereby *become* voices. *The Way to Home* is a symphony of voices.

Speaking the way most of us would if we could, these voices sound out what they have become with compassion, amusement, different angles of vision, and Galvin's unique insights. There is, for example, an Iranian hodcarrier who quietly resists the power of the state; there's the uncle, a priest, who gathers eggs in monastic dawn silence and sends them to the Galvins in wartime Philadelphia. In a poem called "Cream," there are the holy cows as they are known to the girl who milks them, their

> dumb power a gentle hum on the earth,
> making a name by simply being there.
>
> . . . She sees them now, their large heads
> placid and heavy on their settled bodies
> grouped under a tree as if for a painting,
> their browns and whites blending into the soft
> shades of spring the painter has made for them.
> . . . . She means to lie down in their midst,
> the hot flanks breathing on her skin,
> and go to sleep. When she wakes, her face
> will be licked clean and in her hands
> the warm teats will swell and gush.
> She will wash like the queen of hearts in cream.

The girl might not have come up with that lovely line about a yet-to-arrive Dutch painter, but come to think of it, she might have. Note that she is not the speaker, nor is Galvin. The voice is the poem's voice.

While making a poem, Galvin may skid off into a word or phrase just for love of its shock or sizzle. No matter. The poem-in-process can be changed to absorb it. Call it creative process. If it leaves a quiver, I forgive the poet the way I forgive an improvising jazz soloist who hits an off-key note and then uses it instantly to launch a fresh new phrase that extends the melodic line. Hooray! In the cut that follows, notice how the word *threats* leads to *slap* and a change of cadence, easing the poem on its way to home:

> . . . a girl with hair as long
> as winter breath had come up behind and passed
> him on the boardwalk, her bare feet whispering
> threats different and more serious than the slap
> and pause slap and pause of his loose sandals.

There is much joy in the world he gives sounds to, but Galvin is also astonishingly evocative of human inhumanity, even in past wars he never saw. Their distance from him is a challenge. He experiences old wars quickly, but more fully and intently than many on-scene reporters could ever have recorded them. Born in 1937, how could he get the feel of an orphaned girl watching question marks of cranes/planes in the sky over the Warsaw ghetto in 1943? Or "an old woman from County Cork [who] keens/for her sons who fell and broke/in a foreign place called Bloody Lane"?—That's Antietam. Here's another American Civil War voice, that of a soldier, either side will do, saying what he must "After the Battle of Seven Pines":

> Sometimes after the guns had stilled,
> We would hear a girl laugh, the sound
> As strange as frogs in the flour bin.
> Those two days at Seven Pines,
> It seemed as if we forgot how to smile.
>
> Smiling, I figured, was a foreign thing
> That needed muscles I didn't have,
> All of mine gone to hiding out,
> Ducking down, sliding through mud
> That grabbed me with a hundred hands.
>
> I'd like to meet the man from North or South
> Could laugh and mean it after Seven Pines.
> Fair Oaks, some folks call it, but that was later.

He'd have a different place to stand than mine,
Or be a little mad, which I could understand.

The simple truth is, Galvin knows how to ride the currents of words to take him inside almost anything. Call it imagination. He makes voices. The very sounds of words and his passion for mining and arranging them sharpen his social concerns and deepen his sense of history. Call it empathy. These embodied voices called poems are fresh insights into our world and ourselves.

I once hired a kid from the neighborhood to help me unload some heavy boxes of books. He took a quizzical look at the bookcases along the apartment's longest wall and said, "Wow, you got a lot of skinny books." He was noticing the fate of poets in our time: chapbooks, skinny books, almost nothing published that lets them out of the class of frightened 60-page weaklings. It's a memory that prompts me to note that the best poems of Martin Galvin's five earlier books, poems selected by himself, along with 56 gems that are new or newly finished or never before collected, now bask in the full, muscular body that they deserve. Over the years he earned the right to some procrastination about finishing and marketing his fat black notebooks full of manuscripts. Keep in mind that professionally he was that rare thing, a teacher with a PhD who spent his whole career teaching high school kids. That meant that his workload would have required 25 hours a week in classrooms. Compare that to the classroom schedules of poets teaching in colleges —mine if you must—usually nine hours, sometimes only six. But Galvin added still more hours to his teaching; through those many years he taught evening poetry writing workshops at the Writers' Center in Bethesda. He probably would not say that the hours of teaching were at the expense of making poems. I can imagine him studying his students. Notoriously good at teaching, he loved it and knew how to feed the poet he is with the vast and layered experiences of the teacher.

In those many years of teaching, students by the hundreds surely must have said to him, as though it explained or forgave weak writing, *"I'm looking for my voice."* That may be what helped to push Galvin into exceeding his own voice, even in the minority of poems spoken in first person. Whether the speaker is that old textbook omniscient one or a character he invented or Galvin's personal "I," you can feel his frequent, satisfying insistence that a good poem creates its own voice.

I began by saying that there is a poet inside every reader of poems. That inner poet is why you are holding this book in your hands. The poet inside is ready for some conversation, some back-and-forth talk about the poems that are their own voices. I want to end by saying that your inner poet does not have to write poems.

The inside poet—you—is almost ready for some dialogue about the leaps and pleasures of mind that rise from the pages of Marty Galvin's life work. You can talk about how he took you to where you have almost but not quite been before. The voices which are poems are making discoveries about our world and ourselves to which we have no other access. And that to me is the true value of poetry, and why poets write it.

–Rod Jellema

New Poems: 2007-2015

ONE

Advice to the Rose

I would like to address you Rose,
old lady of metaphor, stirring senses
one way or another. I would like,
having offered the traditional honorifics,
Deep-petaled Wonder, Bloom of Kings,
to ask you why, since ancient times,
you keep playing the same dumb joke
on us, and each Spring bloody our hands
and noses for your sweet scent, soft touch.

How many times must your family
laugh at what, you must admit, is a mean trick,
and why, my dear dread rose,
are the points you make so sharp and many,
and why do those points last so long, honed
by the wind, by the snow, by time itself.
I mean, come on Old Girl, a joke's a joke,
and attar matters but the best and the worst
of us can find other ways to heaven.

If you don't behave I'll tell you true,
this modern age we've got the tools:
snappers we got and snippers,
bowls and buckets of rapacious beetles,
and water we can withhold will kill
you dead and dull your contradictions ever more.
Be advised, Dear Fecundity, least worst
of temptresses, Full-blooded most Sweet Thing.
You will get what you need in the deepest deep.
Your red flowers will turn as pale as goat's milk
that stinks of devil's piss. Your thorns, perpetual
as sin, pierce only and always your meager stem.

The Peanut's Underwear

Crack through the rough exterior it shows
To an unkind world that only sees
The peanut as a snack against the pings
A stomach gets before the second inning.
A little pressure with the prehensile thumb
Will get you inside that outside shell
That hasn't fooled a predator for centuries,
Especially not a predator like man.
Get through and you will find a mystery,
The thinnest second line of sheer defense
The peanut mounts against its enemies,
A paper thin diaphanous coat
Around the peanut's heart.
A negligee put on in modesty,
Against invasion, to provoke at least
A scientific inquiry, a naming, a leap
By men most ready to turn the world
And all its parts to their crunching need.

The Boy Could Swim

Gus, whose father's name was Octopusical,
Longed at the bottom of his heart
To study LitraTour in the Ivy League
But was alas wrapped up in seaweed.

Colleges simply dint have the scholars
To teach him what he needed
To be the first of the Octopodes
To write in one of his fine hands
A learned study of, in particular,
English 18th Century LitraTour.

He determined then to spend two
Of his Atlantic years at the art
Of po-Tree and the questions he had
About the stars and toads who made up
Worlds where he would never get nor
Wanted to, being a happy swimmer.

Being a many-handied Octopus, he dreamed
And studied until he started writing himself,
Four poems at a time and all lucid as streams.
The critics loved him for a while. Then,
They learned he had unfair advantage
And treated him heavily, though, truth is,
He never read a word of theirs, nor cared,
Just kept pumping out poems that went beyond,
That showed how a lowly life can be adorned
With lovely words as graceful as his moves,
When no one looked, along the ocean's floor.

Turtle's Way

He was getting tired of following her around
And who did she think she was anyway,
Though the way she waddled through the grass
Changed his irritation to something else
He couldn't name.

He knocked again on her shell, and the beast
Kept going like he wasn't even there, He,
The King of the Ground for miles on end,
Father and Grandfather of his hustling brood
Getting, as usual, no respect

From the turtle lady he'd wooed now
Since she showed she was ready.
She hurried away from him again and again
Until he was at the end of his turtle wits
And his turtle beak was sore from knocking.

How was she going to get eggs worth burying
Unless she remembered standard turtle practices?
He'd polished his technique by watching bulls
In a pasture he'd never think to cross for fear
Of being smashed like a skunk on the county road.

Just turn your back on her, the wise bull showed him,
Just pretend for a moment you don't care for company
That skinny cow'd be under you in a minute,
Backing you into a corner where you want to be.
Or, try the dance your papa showed you. Maybe that'll do.

So here he was, up on his stubby hind legs, dizzy
Enough in a minute he was going to fall on his back
When, as if the chase never happened, she stands
Serene as warm dirt for his clumsy climb,
As ladies can be after a singular message in the sun.

Octopi, Nay Nay

Octopuses are learned guys and girls
Who know when they're being talked about
By ignoramuses who don't know how
To address them with a proper plural.

So if you intend to be a lady or gent
Who knows what's what and when,
Avoid like the plague the fanciful lie
That you were surrounded by octopi

When a fact you can take to the altar is this:
Octopodes may wrap their arms around you
And octopuses kiss you lavishly with lips
You've always hankered after

But when you say you were wooed by octopi,
And taken away to their caves in the deep,
Your father will shake his head and sigh
And your mother will cry and cry.

For there are no such creatures as octopi,
No matter how many the legs and the arms
Swept you away. If you must brag of excesses
Say octopuses or octopodes but never octopi.

A Suburban Creation Myth

I'm a he so she'll be a she for this little telling:
Seems this snake, as quiet and disturbing as the word,
Came sliding up our steps to an outdoor porch,
Where slept the he of this story. She was only in search
Of a little warmth, a bit of a bite to eat, to fit her appetites.

He radiated a warmth somehow snakehood had missed
And besides was covered up with a comforter she coveted.
And so, Why not? She slid inside and cosied-up, the way
Some women will, and went snake-silent to sleep,
Perhaps to dream, and in that dream her hunger rose

And, intuitive as snakes can be, she bit him in the you-
Know-what, for snakes have a way of taking warmth
Wherever it's to be found, in this case, upper thigh.
Her tongue flicked out, as snakes will do, and caught him
Where some dreams and many births by men are made

And brought him straight-upright. She slithered off,
Unsure what she had wrought and he ran in the house
To tell the story of his fallen life to those who would listen
And be sure as angels he was mad as dream-bit man could be.
Then he, who just as well could be a she, slid out of paradise.

Vacuum Cleaners

Once I tried to sell them used,
talked myself door to door,
offering terms. I spent
a couple years like loose change,
rang thankless bells in a fugue state.

The vacuuming I pushed, to tell the truth,
had much to do with my town's crumby kids.
I sold, including all attachments, ten.
I must have moved a couple tons
of demonstration dirt in my career.

Once I guessed I was in love with one,
a blue-bagged Hoover that hummed
and purred and whispered in my ears.
It turned mean in its teens, though,
tried to eat the cat, did eat my daughter's

gerbils. Two. The bulges didn't leave
my eyes for weeks. The sounds of tiny screams
became my ears. I shoved that cleaner clear
down the steps. Airborne at first, it bumped
to earth like a flightless bird, its gravid

belly up to the ears with dirt and death.
I swear I will not ever love another thing
that growls around the house. I've left
the vacuum in the closet, gathering a quiet
dust. Mice nibble nightly at my wired heart.

Explication de Texte

'In order to arrive at what you are not
You must go through the ways in which you are not.'

Thomas Sterns Eliot, *"East Coker"*

I have arrived. I am no aardvark.
And how I know, I went the ways
That Eliot fellow said I ought to go.

Admittedly, I like a crunchy nibble
Of ant dipped in honey as well as most
Of us. I've coaxed my modest snout to grow

Enough to house a tongue that would like to be
An aard's. In McCall's lab I pulled and pushed
Until it ached. All I got for my work was a scar

That stuttered back at me when I checked it out.
I glued a strip of Velcro on the tip of my tongue
To make me more efficient at the craft

Should my appetites decide I'd best be served
By sniffing those termite mounds and anthills
To satisfy my ache to feed among the better

Beasts. My tongue had trouble staying off
The roof of my mouth. Through such practices
I have come to an important truth of being:

The *I who am* is no ant-eating aardvark boy.
Now in the case of the kangaroo it's trickier
because I like to jump around a lot, and, too,

I have always found pouches dandy things.
I wonder did that old poet man know how big
A beast I've got not to be before I be an *am.*

The Octopus in Charles Dickens' Work

He wrote so many letters, Charles Dickens,
he kept an octopus as ink supply.
Sometimes, when he grew as weary as the moon,
Charles Dickens had his octopus
Write his letters for him. True, he dictated them
at first. Four at a time, the octopus could write,
And if he had some paper-weights, eight.

An octopus is very smart and doesn't live long.
If he is to be useful he has to work fast.
Have you ever seen the baby octopi swim
Out of its mother's womb? Slick and fast.
Charles Dickens knew from reading *Hard Times*
How hard sometimes a woman must work
For nothing much, for some scrapings
Off the sea's bottom, for the chance to see
Her babies for their moment in the hungry world.

Music in Dickens' world can be compared
To the music in Shakespeare's plays, but not
To advantage if you happen to be an ABD.
One octopus, for example, can play at once
the flute, the clarinet, French horn and kazoo
To a spontaneous crescendo only paralleled
By the mobs of freed-men storming the Bastille.
Muted, granted. Much music is unheard.
Dickens used that knowledge well
In his little tales of two cities, yours and mine.

Octopuses wear their soft bodies on the outside,
their souls are dry. It is known that Dickens
had a dry soul in his writing life.
When he toured, the soul got wet and sloppy
So he only toured when he needed money.

Where Corsages Grew

As Irish and as simple as a potato
The girl who was my best pal
In high school (though now her name
Is buried someplace in my brain
Where I can't reach it anymore
Than I can grow a daisy out of pistol shot)
Lived in a sunny house beside the cemetery
Where flowers bunched in sympathy
Just begging for some human use.

Gladiolas there were, and roses without thorns,
Great splashes of carnations as if the dead
Had proms coming up of their own.

One of the reasons she was my best pal
And, in fact, the best pal of every girl
Going to the Senior Prom that year
Was her easy access to those grave flowers
And her having no fear of the bones
We were still sure, being country girls,
Would wrap themselves around us
If we went walking through that place at night
Being pretty good looking girls as well.

She'd wait until the moon came up
And the wolves between us and Scranton howled
Then for the solid week before the prom
She'd gather corsages before they were made
And in the day she'd shape them up
So not even we could believe they came from graves
Because beside being good-looking we
Were fairly simple too and glad to dance
At the only Senior Prom we ever hoped to see
This side of where she'd swiped those flowers
For our sheer delight from the great uncaring dead.

Tattoos

Since I am old enough to have a history,
gastric and spinal juices rush, in their delicate vials,
through important rooms where things happen.
Those glimmering liquids though, being invisible
Have little say about the who I would like to be
Since I am old enough to have a history.

They, in my bare-skinned mind,
Equal the hairless, deflated chest,
Insignificant to the matter at hand,
which is making a mortal show of myself
my teenage immortality, my vital need
to have a picture punched into my arm,
a legend etched above each nipple.

mort, mortable, unimmortal, morcurial,
the etching in Palmer Method, the essential
who, the *reductio ad absurdum* of others,
ideas beyond the competence of juices,
ideas to be dealt out by the bald headman,
for the summary sum of five days' wages,
up front and no kidding around.

Having such a history has advantages.
One learned wit, bred on latin, has inscribed "Sic
Semper............. on my prostate,
leaving the operative noun,
the telling, accusatory subject blank,
for another wise one and another time to finish off.

Tattoos, that modicum of literacy left as legacy
to our generation, and exercised by numbing artists
in seaports everywhere, have now become my own.
Born To Swill, I've punched above my left nipple.
Sworn To Skin above my right. In brotherly love,
my toes squeal and grunt inside the shoe-sties
where they ride to market to buy some more mud.

Other things I've written elsewhere on myself,
scars for one, and lines, lines of age everywhere -
across the knuckles, up the palm
and around the thumb, across the forehead,
across the heart, among the capillaries,
among the veins, lines sometimes on lines.

There's a woman in Cleveland makes her living
reading lines off working men. She wouldn't
trace what my lines are saying, no sirree.
There's a woman in Duluth though, she knows
what my lines are telling me to do tonight
which is written inside the artery where I'm
always losing my pulse, and the scalpel
the doctor would like to use to get at it.
I've the appointment etched to remind me
Where I can't see nor want to.

PG-13

There's got to be a good girl
And a bad guy or a good guy
Who is lost in the turgly woods
While the good girl pines
And the bad guy slobbers and slavers,
Thinking like crazy of the good girl,
Or, very occasionally, a bad bad girl
Who mostly has a desire to kill good guys
And bad guys without discrimination.

The audience, should there be one,
Will be composed of good guys and girls
Wanting to be a little bad and some bad guys
With good girls trying to save them.
In the audience we invite to pay for the pleasure,
There are no bad girls. The really bad guys
Who slaver and slobber will be barred
From attending for fear they will have
Malicious and viscious and very bad diseases
By the attendant who looks like a cross
Between Chang Kai-shek and Mary Magadalene.
Popcorn hulls ache a little like the end of youth.

The Way Things Accumulate

Here's the way that things accumulate.
You're in a place seems right. You're six.
You fall down, hit your head, the blood
bumps along the ground like a model train.
You're out. First time away since the womb.

You wake up, something's changed. You.
The place. The world. Everything. Enough
for you to know but not to say. Enough
you know you're on your way. Next time,
you're sixteen. We all know kids. Try anything.

Port wine for you, right into the empty place.
You wake up, something's changed. Subtle.
The shades are drawn across the moon
a different way, for one. The ocean hits
the beach a little harder than it did.

Little stuff you don't even know you know
but say, or begin to, anyway. And then
your father hits his head on blind
concrete that doesn't look where he's going.
Not quite dead, but emptied out, dead enough

not to come back the way he went away.
Your mother mothers him. His wife dies. His sons
become him. Nothing remains and everything's
the same, the ways that things accumulate.
You wake up, something's changed.

Sounds maybe. Not enough to hear, but there.
One knows. You know these things.
Once in your twenties, you pass out
for want of something better to do.
You know what it's like in your twenties,

things accumulate. Anyway, you wake up,
It's a different place. Askew. Awry.
Afloat. Adrift. O.K., but cosmic chaos,
Dig? So now you're one-two-three-four worlds
away from where you started. More or less

the same as anyone your age, calamity
Next, your taste buds atrophy. Not many, mind,
one or two, but there are some things you can name
more surely than you will ever taste again.

Burbles of gingerale, for one. Remember them?
And nibs that smacked of dirty knuckles?
The ways that things accumulate for gain.

And there are more worlds too and faster gained
as you go on. Your older daughter, younger than
she thinks, tries a flying leap, backward,
from the monkey bars that part the sky and parts
her hair too deep for rinsing out. The doctor

wakes her up. Another doctor puts your wife to deepest
elsewhere so he can take away what works too well
(her galled bladder) announcing it's not working.
And then it's everybody's losses that you gather up
in bushel baskets. The little passing out, the faints,

the cold explosions in the surgery, the accidents
that change the world unceasingly, you gather in
like snow, like trees, like breath. No world,
not one, the same and gathered richness all around.

Come, wash yourself in the snow as trees do,
wash in the charged air as breath does. Take
what you've got. In another day, You'll have more
and better too, the way that things accumulate.

Risibility

A laugh can be a knife, a club, a breeze
From April's Riviera, a stet gun
Stuttering its fear that it shall leave
Anyone here to laugh.

A laugh is a cough, a trill, a shriek,
A bark, surely a bark.
A laugh is a punch in the ear,
A jab in the kidneys, hard.

There's a town in Kansas hates
A laugh as bad as a drought.
Generations of boys there dream
That a clown's laughing face

Means to eat them alive.
In houses there a laugh's a razor
That tears freckles off the face.
Another town, another place

That's fed for years on fatback,
A laugh's a Papal blessing,
A needle and thread for the heart,
A guggle of good in a dry well.

I've seen a girl there torn in half
By other girls giggling up their sleeves
At what she wore, at what she said
And didn't. She's a laugh, that girl.

The laugh's on you, I've heard,
The laugh's on me. You think
It's accidental people have trouble
Remembering jokes? That's a laugh.

There's not an echo of that word
I'd give as gift: snicker, cackle,
Hee-haw, guffaw, snigger, snort.
When you hear a thing like that, run for it.

The Seer Sees

I said to the seer See
And he cried but I am blind

I said to the wise man Speak
And he signed but I am dumb

I said to the loudmouth Quiet
And he laughed me down the stars

I said to myself Be Still
And I danced the jig of the mad

I said to myself Be mad
And I cried but I am man

The seer said See I told you so
The wise man spoke in circles

The loudmouth snored at the sky
And I cried but I am man.

Practicing the Rhetoric

Getting's a lovely sound and notion.
Consider the joy of gathering the thing itself,

the quid of quiddity: getting a job,
for instance, getting a woman to wife,

getting a man worth a good woman's time.
Consider then the opposite, the got,

the sloven who over beer will brag,
Today, Man, I got laid. I got to go.

I have got the answer to the birth
of the universe. I really have got

the perfect kid. You know, the kind
you'd like to have but don't?

To him who got, we mostly wish
a getting gone, back to his hovel

and, having once been got, that he get
no more of his misbegotten kind

they being surely a surly redundancy
that will be forgotten as fast as begotten.

Getting's enough, we hope,
to get us toward where we're going next

TWO

Medical Student

She pores over the bones and guts of her text,
drinking skim *grande latte* at the cafe,
one hand clenched around the handle
as if it were her anatomy teacher's throat,
one hand around a yellow magic marker.
She needs the marker's presence
to get her through this book, to meet
the stomach-churning test that is
a monthly check on her progress.

She means to score each defining word
onto her wrinkled brain, the high-lighter
an etching pen. She hopes the gene
that carries color-blindness isn't on her DNA.
Her fingers though, they ache for the scalpel,
need something to remind her. An alchemy
figures in her yellow, burning maybe miracles
on to the gray and sleepy dross of her brain.

She's not sure yet about the brain's chemistry
but she has heard it's fond of gold. She plans
to spend this year making hers glisten, synapses
sparking and lighting it up like the first 4th of July
she spent with her boyfriend while the sky made stars .

Immigrant, Working Chickens

He makes his living chasing chickens
In the scalding skinning gutting place
The Owner calls the Fowl Processing House.

Scant money, too, for running down those birds.
Somebody had to to keep the place in shape.
He wouldn't do those other jobs for anything.

This is the life he was meant for as a boy,
Why he became so good at football that depended
On footwork, fastwork, endurance and some guts,

Knowing how to shake loose of a defender
Take a pass cutting for the goal and score.
When he's home, he wouldn't touch a chicken

Though he brings home the ruined ones for free
so the kids, his wife and his madre can eat
the way he used to back in the old country.

There's no applause for a chicken chaser
In the slaughterhouse and when he takes his wages
Home, no cheers. And when he takes his Friday bath,

There's not a soap alive can scrub the loss away.
Sometimes he runs the pattern of the doomed
With his eyes shut, as if he had no eyes, no brain

To think things through the way a chicken does
With his head cut off. You close your eyes
To guess their moves and chase them down.

The ones that get loose before they arrive
At the chicken chopper's station, they're the ones
Cause most of the trouble on the line. Once a shift
he lets them pretends they're faster than he is,

Gives them a couple extra breaths for free
The way he'd want his boys to have before
What has to be will be. Now and then

One makes it out the door. He lets it go.
A man can't be expected to catch them all, he figures.
That's what he figured crossing over, what he prayed.

House Call With Violin

This doctor man comes up to me and grins,
So how's the leg, it feeling any better? And then
He gets this sad and happy face, looking at

My baseball glove and out of left field, says,
Boy, how about the sounds that you hear inside?
You ever want to get that music out and singing?

I tell you, davey-boy, I thought the guy was whack-o,
Like my Uncle Paul who gave me a Louey-ville once
And said, Now you can hit like Ted Klezewski.

After that, it got worse, then better, the way things do.
The doctor said, Look here, I'll give this fiddle to you
Free for nothing and a month of lessons from Mrs. Crouch.

You only have to promise to let those inside sounds out
By practicing like crazy twice a week right before supper.
By the second lesson I knew I had a violin,

And I had to hide it from my Pa because… you know.
So I did—for the secret of it. Those cats.
The one scooted up that old oak like he was a squirrel

when I played those first notes as sour as biting a lemon.
The other jumped the fence and chased himself to town
and back in a hurry. No wonder. More dogs there

than that old General Mills has oats in its pantries.
Every time I get that violin zinging though, I think
I hit a grand slam homer, last of the ninth.

I hear that doc has done the same for a bunch of boys.
You ought to get to be his patient. What the heck,
Maybe he'd fork over a piano with a stool that spins

Your Nancy right into a waltz. Maybe you'd even learn
To dance. Wouldn't that be a hoot? Me bowing the violin
And you dancing on home plate trying to strike out.

Umbilicals: An Ecumenical Guide for Boys

For James Joseph

Grow an extra foot next year before the parents
Look and have a word with you about your habits.
They can be as tedious as violins, parents.

Once a week for a season or two make calls
To no one you know on your mother's calling card.
Dial 1, then any random set of ten numbers. Ten.

Repeat until you get through to a tiny voice. Speak
Pidgin Mandarin no matter who says what? Where?
Who is this anyway? Let them hang up first.

In fact, once you make contact, don't let them hang up
At all. Sing them a song of sixpence with a Gaelic lilt
If they insist that no one there speaks Mandarin.

Remember parents, those music masters. They want you
To grow up sane and seemly as if the sane don't eat bananas
Like the rest of us, as if the seemly don't ravel themselves

Inside their clothes and spend therefore hours in closets
And stores and doctor's offices. Even milk teeth are negotiable
With parents. So can be a threat of hair they can't control.

Practice saying this: "If you don't let me (choose one),
I'll paint a mustache on my shirt. I'll go to church
And sing hard rock, I will." Later in the game, fourth quarter,

Score tied, do so. Maybe at the Feast of Pentacost.
After that, You're on your way. Enough of games and ruses.
You know the numbers to punch out on any phone you're near.

Remember though, Mandarin. No matter how your mother weeps
In her soup for you, your father swears on a stack of your own
Peanut-buttered piano exercises. Mandarin. And don't hang up.

Undergraduate Days

Freshman year I was Don Quixote,
was one of the four hundred
riding boldly and well, was Kevin Barry
on his way to death that morn.

'Then, deciding not to die for a while,
I moved to sophomoric sophistication,
knew I knew better than my older sister.
Found a path I didn't even know I'd lost,
a way through a life of haughty women
and lonely men leaning on lampposts.

I was a singer then, so I roared
let's get it on, you and I, let's go
through midnight's mutterings
and arrive where we started,
knowing it for the first time.

But then I tired of this round-about
and took, my Junior summer, a path
most traveled by world weary men,
a path to heaven by the way of hell
and became a sinner of the nth degree.

Senior year, a time of final circularity
and serious talk with serious minds,
I took the bar exam and whiskey straight,
I vowed I'd never come this way again,
My cap and gown shrunk my voice to size.

The King's English

For the Gatherer of the OED, Will Murray

For the first time in all his wife's talking,
Will Murray heard the broad dialect
Of her birth town as she lay dying.

He forgot to cry foul, almost forgot to grieve,
as he puzzled out the place of her soundings,
consulted his collection of cards about the chance

that what she spoke had not been heard
for two hundred years, as if the world
in its goodbyes is better said in old tongues,

as if the whole book of the words
might need new shaping, with an eye and an ear
for the ways the future remembers and forgets.

New fruit from old roots so deep in the dirt
takes time to ripen and grow sweet.
There are words inside the deep silence,

Will Murray, the great silence of her going.
There are consolations found in the ebb
of retreating tides, heard as the riptide

Says *I am* to the swallowing sea,
To be seen in the words you stayed to name
And the ones you'd never be old enough to hear.

Fingering a Way to Count

For Sarah Caitlin, the clencher

I've an index finger to point things out,
To track the alphabet of my ways and means,
To keep the book on what I have and have not got.

Sometimes, that finger bends to touch the thumb,
To say I am man, no lesser mammal I,
With ways to grasp beyond the ken of lesser apes,

I make and shred at will, I beckon GO
And oceans yield to the command, the sky
Itself promises to hold me up and does.

I've one finger that can pull a trigger,
Three to guide a brush to make a likeness
Beyond imagining, five that can say Halt

And mean it, five that can run around a back
That isn't even mine and make it purr.
I will these fingers to my kids and my kids' kids.

When they're working out the ways to count
They can unfurl those fingers one by one
And bring what's true into the clenching sun.
And hide what counts from the clenching sun.

What Google Didn't Know

Styptic Pencil :56% aluminium sulfate

My father was a tough little man
      who hated styptic pencils.
He flushed one down the toilet and it got stuck
      and pretty soon the plumber came,
            said it was like a beaver dam and no wonder.

So when my father cut himself shaving, made a few
      of those little nasty nicks that looked, to a boy,
like death, he'd paste tiny tears of toilet paper
      against the blood. Most times, that flimsy stop
            would save the family from the disaster

of his missing the local train that carried him
      from across our street down to Port Richmond
and his job of yelling at large men about shifting freight.
      He always wore a suit and tie to sanctify his words
            and by the time he came home the cuts were healed.

Soon as he got on the morning train,
      I'd go upstairs and put bits of toilet paper
all over my face then run to my mother to get
      some sympathy. They'd never stick like his
            but float down to their moments of surrender

so I knew I'd never be a railroad man,
      nor wear a white shirt my wife would iron
in the kitchen after dinner. And I'd never get to yell
      in a voice bigger than myself about my day
            while my kids gaped in hunger at the noise.

I keep a styptic pencil on my desk to keep count
      of all the cuts I did not have to stay before I went
to tame my teen-aged classes. I never shout
      but oh the look I've mastered from my mother's look
            can staunch a galoot as quick as a stick of styptic.

Hanging Out

There are not a lot of places to hang around
Anymore. The corner mail box where we sat
Has gone downtown. The ice cream counter
At the local pharmacy, its circling stools,
Gone. We used to go to bowling alleys
For the careful pleasure of making the spare,
The certain way the explosion of ten pins
Was just enough of violence. And church,
A good place for hanging out when you're 12
And needing the bloodburn of a flowering blush
When she walked down the aisle and sat
May god be praised, a pew and a half away.
She smelled like Easter Saturday, violet and innocence
Setting up a sweet confusion between faith and hope.
I like to think of puzzling places now, list what's less
Lonely than computers, discover where to stay
And where to go to bring me back to where I was.

Southern Matinee, Reprise

The pistons were at the heart of it, taking the father's car
and the family the straight way from Baltimore's Brooklyn
neighborhood to Florida despite our mother's heebie-jeebies.
That sedan slicked us through the smoke of a wild fire

smack into a thin Georgia town's radar trap.
The Daddy-O was as smooth as the greased comb
he ran through the two-wave pompadour.
Belly to belly, he talked his way around a cop
with an accent could have slowed us down for good,

then talked us into motels wouldn't have us otherwise.
"White trash," I heard one woman call us in a voice
as thick and slow as Tuesday morning. My father
didn't bother sassing back but turned away and kissed
my mother right smack on the mouth. Better

than ever, he said, and grinned his crazy smile,
as full of teeth, as right, as the friendly dragon
in last month's matinee who was about to die
and roared the way dragons are supposed to
to save himself and made me as glad as Saturday.

That roar, that kiss, those pistons pumping,
made me remember too what I'd just as soon
forget about this new year's main feature,
How I'm left to puzzle at my heart that attacked itself
and danced for joy at nothing I could see, then eased

me across four lanes of interstate, to park itself
and me and the car on the weedy verge and wait
with the snakes for the rescue squad to come
and the cop whose breath smelled of stale beer
tired out from chasing a shot of rye.

Had my Daddy been here, he'd have yelled
for love's sake to get a son's blood up to racing
like a stock car around a dirt track, chasing
itself in a circle, the parts going faster than reason,
the traffic parting for the hot blood's gushing river.

Circus Matinee

Remember the clown who jumped into the lap
of your mother the moment the blue elephant
paraded in. Remember how you wet
your pants crying about that clown and what
he was doing on the mother's lap and then
laughing so you wet them again. Remember that?

And father got ticked at you about
being a baby when you were almost five
and besides he wanted to watch the clowns pile out
of the tiny car, not drag a galoot of a kid
to the can. And the mother smiled at Gunther
the tiger tamer, the popcorn jumped out of the bag.

the father went in to the Army and didn't come back,
and you never wet your pants again, not once.
Remember that? Remember how you cried?

The Romantic's Day in Arizona

The fifth driver that he flags pulls over, leans
across to open the right door of her pickup truck.

Her smile cracks and spreads like a goose egg
in the ninth inning of a no-hitter. He wonders
why it is she looks so happy, this is serious,
this being in a lonesome place with nothing doing
but the coyotes pitching their hunger at him,
this could be the end of what he knows as music.

He wonders why it is his voice cracks open
and spills the syllables into the cabin ahead of him,
what he will do if she should pull a knife,
tell him to strip and hurry up about it too,
how the turkey buzzards will circle in
above the body she leaves behind, her exhaust
a chain of evidence drifting into the desert night,
what she will do with the part of him she takes
away. "Going as far as Tucson," she says.

"Good I saw you. A girl needs company crossing over."
"Oh, yeah," he thinks, and climbs in anyway, just his luck
he picked this time of day to watch the sun set
over purple mountain's majesty, just his blinking luck.

Visual Aids At the Finishing School

My student, seventeen and safe again,
brings in a knife to show the class
how she got through a couple years
of early high school in Sri Lanka

She also brought back to suburbia
the exotica of Arabia which she wears
as if she were a native there, not here.
The blade contains a promise of bright death,

hidden in a scabbard that is no
less bold, declares: *I hold safe*
the sharpness of the world. There is always
something to be hidden in what we keep

to let loose on those who would be close.
She wears a sari in the ancient way.
The boys, schooled on girls who want to be others,
whet their appetites with ancient thoughts.

THREE

Vocabulary for a Marriage

For Tara and Greg

First, the words you won't miss, not a bit,
do this, do that, dry up, chill out
all the clipped imperatives that cut
the heart out to make the mind behave.
Take your medicine.
Mind your manners. Think.
And all the words you won't need this time around
I don't, I won't, I can't, No, Not me. No way.

The verbs you'll find inside the cake,
inside the rings, inside the hearts
of us who'd rather have you not behave
are today's and tomorrow's words,
the words you'll make all month.
All year if you can help it, if you can help
yourselves to a language fit for anytime.

Such words sound around the place like echoes
of the heart. *Love*, they say, and *Give*
and *Wait. Wonder* and *Wander* and *Play*.
And always, everywhere, the merry yells
of *Yes*, and *Yes* roll through your rollicking world.

The pronouns that you'll need, you give
ourselves as gift. You give you *Us* and *We*
You take away for good the straight backed
pride of *I*, the blind authority of *they*,
the greedy *me*, and *me* and *me*.
Today, you give each other *You*
and doing so, you give us back ourselves.

A Way to Home

My way to home's a silly hill,
The climb an easy one, full of releases,
Long as I want. And when I reach
To top, the way down's gentler still

Though set with cunning traps,
A gopher hole, moldy logs that hide
Their troubles, mirages in the distance:
Men I've known, a water hole with lion.

I take my time. I'm no Sisyphus
To be hurried along by what I cannot bear.
I know a hill's the way to go from home,
The little struggles bring their own rewards,

A broken arm that taught me how to medicate,
A snake that taught me how to circle fear,
Fantasies that put reality in its place
The joy of taking pebbles from my shoes.

Longevities:

After Jan Steen's *The Dancing Couple 1663*

The air beneath her heel has waited
three centuries to be stirred to lift her.

She is wearied out the way old ladies get
from being stepped around and curtsied to,

would like some courtly action, so when
the man kicks down his heels and walks

toward her, as bright as April sunshine on
the cobblestones, urging the great drays

to the lug-tug task they put their haunches to,
she wants, despite the time, to dance.

That singular man wakes her toes to fling
responses others can not see and have nothing

much to do with work except the work of their
standing still while dancing together, getting them

up and down the centuries as fully as Steen
and their dream allow them to be imagined.
Allows them to be still stilly moving.

Adolescence of the Artist

The first teen-ager of *homo sapiens*
to growl a threat away from her or else
had meant only to clear her throat to beg for mercy.
Barring that, to pray that the end would happen
since it had to, fast, that the pain not be too bad.

Her fingers told her it was time
to empty her head of the strange goings-on
inside, so she found a cave full of the dark
she fed on for its own sake, a place she loved,
and seeing another animal inside her eye,
she picked a handy wall and carved him there.

Eclipse and the Young Artist at Lescaux

The night wolf is eating the baby light again.
      The last time that happened, you disobeyed
           And went alone into the big dark.
We thought the night wolf's whelp had you
      In their den. We thought that you had gone
           Over the breath mountain to a place beyond,
That your life was chosen to replace the taken.

Now you have chipped at our cave wall
      And an animal we do not know stares
           Always onto our food and into our sleep
As if the night wolf eats again.
      Go now outside and pray to the Light God
           That he throw his spears at the night wolf
So we may be safe in the time before he comes to stay.

Let his deep grumble of a voice scare the wolf away.
      Pray that he speak soon that we may be forgiven.

First Cousins at the Gallery

My father tells me about the paintings,
how they slip their hooks when no one
but the kid with the peg leg's looking.

Off the wall they come, he says,
Sick to death of hanging there with all
their warts sticking out like bullfrogs.

He only means to scare me away
From what he calls a ballet-dancer life.
He says the paintings have to grin and bear it,

take the days like heavyweight champs.
The kids in my class spending their museum day,
oohing and *aahing* at bloody battle scenes.

I guess the books are cousins to the paintings,
have known them since they were kids,
have mutual enemies and memories.

My father would have preferred I knew them
Not at all, had spent my days at fire-fighting
So we could all live safe inside ourselves.

The paintings remember the crisp night
light after dull day. The books remember how
words burn, admire a sudden blaze of light.

Second Light at the Uffizi

The cobblestones of Florence
trip me up as they have hobbled men
and horses these thousand years
in the narrowed-down streets.
Above my head and the *Pieta's*,
the derricks fight the sun for space.
Nobody laughs or cries about my fall
except my ankle. Just kidding,
it would say if it had tongues,
just showing what an ankle's made to do.

Bones and joints, I build myself into the air
Again above the stones of Florence,
learning what it is to know
the shades of gray that ground
a person down can lighten up
his hurtling heart. Later today
the sun will show me how to paint
the town, the derricks will dance
me toward the upper air.
The very stones will take on light.

Black and White

Barnett Newman at the National Gallery

Barnett Newman
dipped himself in paint as penance,
and took eight years to make
his Stations of the Cross.

Found magna
for the first two stations: simple things,
something like a human life,
a little blur of a vertical shape which may
or may not be the real stuff of pain, a few bits
of a softened black paint on the ivory canvas,
the canvas made a cream that gushed
onto our blank lives, and, perhaps, all
we needed of terror and all we had of love.

1958 and things just starting to perk up
in America coming on to the down
hill side, the slalom that would take our breath away.
Two down and twelve to go and all the time
in the world, all the time he had left and willing
to use, on canvases that might be confused
with blank shells, might be mistaken for a snow
job, one of those things those *artistes* do
and hoity toity make fools of us who do
the real work in this U.S. of A.

Makes you wonder
how a man could use what's left of his life
doing such a thing, twelves all around him,
and nothing else to do for the life of him,
as if that were enough, a counting out, as if
he knew the figure was beyond imagining.

Museum Guard

He is pulled pell-mell inside the frames,
onto the canvases, splayed, a minor figure
in any scene he has before him,
a minor figure spent beside what lives.

Like nothing else, museum walks exhaust
his only mortal muscles, that recently had
moved him at engrossing speeds around
a jogging track. Museum rooms dwarf

and drown his heart in paints, have no regrets.
A pastoral scene can draw the strength
from him, drain thought, compel attention.
He needs to be swallowed by the liquid eyes

Factoring

Because the paintings will not yield their colors up,
because we want to wrinkle up the easy circles of our lives,

because the girl's neck leans, precarious and precise,
toward the boy who would rather kiss than comfort her,

because our cups and saucers will not break before we do,
we work ourselves into the cupboards of the painter,

memorize the glaze of earth and sky from which he drinks,
write things down we didn't know we know,

pause inside the music, inside the artist's eye,
watching the boy who would rather not

appear on the canvas be there anyway
and, poised on the edge of himself will lean,

precarious and precise, toward the girl
because that is what we want to remember to want,

because the artist remembers that angle of repose,
because we, who have other things to do, who factor out

most things, will spend today at the gallery, factoring in
what needs to be for us to be as sane as the painting.

Finding Harmony:

After Waiting for Godot

I am tired of being less than what
I am and so, my friend, are you.

We have been comrades too long
To be short with each other,

Weak too often when it counted most
To be strong when it mattered least.

I am often happy to be less than I am
And so are you, *mon frere, mon ami.*

We have cried in relief, you and I,
We have laughed in our grief.

There have been times when time lagged
Like a coward, ran like the deer

You almost shot but couldn't.
Time when time began for us

And time when it began to end.
But it always ends before it begins,

The way we count, the way the hands sweep
Minutes into hours that stop at 12

And move like us, my friend, toward one.
This is not that, but could be,

This tired of being tired, proud
Of exhaustion, breathless and bold.

We are happy to be more than we are,
You and I, placid, at peace in our pain.

For the Ever-Afters

If only they had left the soft parts under ice
to present to us, a bit of the pituitary,
some of the old gray matter, a liver or two,
we might know better where they came from,

how they loved and fed and fell into the *sapiens*
we call ourselves. But all we have are a few bones,
some incisors, to say this ancestor had no dentist
and a history that goes right back to baby teeth.

He must have had a caring mother who set
the odd fracture from the looks of it.
We hope the scientists to follow us have better stuff
to work with: frozen brains, the weight of the soul

as it flew off, the ratio of birds we saved to the men
we killed because they never learned to fly,
so the Ever-Afters can guess how we lived,
how honored, how happy we were to die.

FOUR

V-E Day

For Paul

V-E Day broke on May and Wadsworth Avenue
and made me rich. Old men with nobbled knees
ssued from their front doors, waving paper money
jingling silver dollars, to get the *Extra! Extra!*
I crowed like a strut of rooster. My brother

as the donkey. I fed him penny candy
to keep on toting papers and promised freedom
and enough dough to get him to an A's game
at Shibe Park. By the time that we were done,
the dark night was almost over. Since I

was ten, I bought myself a big cigar at the drug
store, said it was for my uncle coming home
from beating up the Sauerkrauts, and gathered
my little brother's pals in pow-wow
so I could tell about the ways of men at war.

As I puffed great O's and they watched me
with mouths agape, I got one story out that Ernie Pyle told
to Walter Winchell and all the ships at sea about a boy
who'd died at Normandy a hero for us all before
I got sick half almost to death and had to go to confession

the next day for several grievious offenses
and not a bit of sanctifying grace to help me
with the belly ache that lasted longer than the smoke.
The kids went home and told their moms
who told mine who didn't much care and to prove it

gave me and my sour mouth a washing down.
Fels Naptha, that brown scorch of everything adult
that kids had to take, defined the rest
of that day and the European Theater for me.
A month before, when Roosevelt died, I made

my first fortune, my brother learning his place
I shouted out surprise and grief the old men bought
The same way that they would buy the joy of victory.
Next day, the little twerp took the money I gave him
for doing what I wouldn't, being older and the boss.

Took the money and bought my mother father
the sister my brothers and me
a case of tincan quarts of grapefruit
from Braun's, the corner grocer, who had
his private war to fight, being Kaiser bred

and the whole neighborhood to convince.
A case of grapefruit juice. I wonder still what
the twerp was thinking. When I belch now
the acid of that still climbs up vines
inside me, who would have made an ace marine.

Battle Dress

I'm going out to buy some combat boots
And put them on each night before the evening
News so I can be prepared to do

A little listening in the line of duty
I know there's miles to go before the tingle
Of getting there to buy some combat boots.

I'll lace them up inside my living room
And limber up my idle fingers
So I will better be prepared to do

The dishes, scrub the pots when dinner's through.
I'll do my push-ups, make my muscles sing,
And head on out to buy my combat boots.

I'll have them painted red and white and blue.
And wear them to my church. The bells will ring
Out loud to see that I'm prepared to do

What's needed. When the going's rough, I go,
Though the truth is I would rather linger.
So I'm going out to buy my combat boots.
What's to be done, I am prepared to do.

Twilight at Arlington

There's little enough to like about a war:
Some graceful lines to a fortification,

Little things, practical, ephemeral,
The pleasures one gets from working well,

But men at war, men scared and scarred,
Are beautiful in their just being there,

The least and the best as beautiful as birth.
We come to Arlington in blood allegiance

To them who held the bleeding heads of friends
on laps blood-soaked. Lord, let the grass be soft

in Arlington, connect what was with what will be,
for what they hazarded and what we lost,

Where boys play sandlot ball and the runner
Caught in a rundown is always safe at home

Headstones

The headstones tell no stories, standing there
All prim and proper, attended by the yardsmen,
The stones have nothing at all to say, even
To the winds, who keep continual on this hill to teach,

Us grief, the stones tell no stories, but the names do
The names say what would have been
Had they lived their life. The machinist McCabe
Who meant to discover things about the wheel,

Rogers, who ran the mess with an iron hand,
Who could have cut new ways into space and time.
The ship's carpenter Collins who whistled off tune
His father's favorite, a doleful "Mother Macree"

Who would have written a Newer World Symphony
As quiet as the mating dance of butterflies,
As subtle as the first egg of a fertile lady.
But this is no time for rapture, no time for beginnings,

No time more for sadness writ large and cold
As letters on a dead man's crypt. It is a time,
A place for memory to see the way
The single tree fell, finding its slow way

Between the arms of its parents, its brothers,
Its children and cousins, to meet the quiet call
Of gravity, a fall that required more than one
Letting go, that I will remember all the forest long.

Civil War Reenactment

To celebrate an obscure battle
in a most uncivil war, the town next door
to ours puts on, for the citizens' edification,
a slice of death in the 1860s.

The town baker is there, dressed up
as Johnny Reb, with a musket and yell
for dying well. The pharmacist stands tall
with his ramrod behind the ancient cannon
that still made noises. What a time it is!

Popcorn and firecrackers for the kids,
Old time photo ops for Mom and Dad,
a great chance to glower and holler hell's-
a-popping for folk most often given
to whispers about the neighbors' sex-life

and cracking wise about the celebrity
who got off easy while you and me
would have been slapped in jail
for years and a day for a lousy mis-
demeanor: pain by motor vehicle

while under the misfluence of a busy bee.
The stovepot bubbles through carrots and corn
as if they were cousins. Symmetry attends
most of the ladies' eyes though some, we have heard,

are struck by the devil's fork and look crooked
upon peace and harmony. The men go on
as men must, practicing the use of the bayonet
when the red-eyed enemy stops by to dance.

Boys tote buckets of water for car radiators
and big girls blush and flutter their bosoms
at the soldiers who would only be soldiers
for this particular slice of death before they return
to their everyday of sweating little and smiling much.

A Sensible Sleep in Time of War

Last night, I talked again
With the headless man in knickers
Who had a point to make about the war
I did not care to hear.

I tossed him aside, as I have the right
And turned to face myself in the dark
That swallowed shadows and hid the blood
I did not care to see.

For a moment or two I was content,
Or at least was not at war with myself.
But then I saw the more than mortal man again,
I did not care to touch,

For who can help a bloody man
Who speaks in a tongue unforked and soft,
And offers bread, and offers wine
I can not bear to taste.

I stopped my breath for the time it took
To lose him for good in the night.
And I dreamed of the smell of snow,
Flowers of horseradish diced to delight,

And all of us sane and all of us whole.
Heads on our shoulders, toes on our feet.

FIVE

A Stand of Eucalyptus

I will not remember
The smell of eucalyptus,
The dull roar and whine
Of the indifferent chain saw
Biting through the legs
Of the dense stand.

But to see the way
The single tree fell,
Finding its slow way
To meet the quiet call
Of gravity, a fall
That required more than one
Letting go,
That I will remember
All the forest long.

English Sparrows

Balanced on the footbridge
across the narrowed lake
in St. James's Park,
a stern-mouthed London man
weighed exactly five sparrows
on the wit of one opened hand.

Birdseed made his palm a field.
"Amazing," I said, "Truly remarkable thing.
How long'd that take," I asked,
"to train those birds to trust a man to be
a field?" He looked at me as if my words
were dust, moon talk on steady English soil.

He stared at the single sparrow whose fear
had made it dull and useful, feeding
on the mites who underate the bridge.
I turned away, toward more language
than I had. Ten yards farther on,
four girls from somewhere else

balanced exactly twenty sparrows
on a farm of hands. A fifth girl watched,
afraid to try her self until she saw me
watching her, afraid. Then she stretched
her arms onto the sounding air and called
for something in a tongue that worked.

The sparrows settled on her like a dark
dream. Their craws were pink plows,
sheathed and shining. I said to her,
"Just astounding," I said. "Really something."
Her look said, "You're as dreary as a pencil."
I turned away, palms up, and prayed for rain.

Little Bones

The moon this year is worth the waxing.
Spare us badger teeth and turmoil
In the neighbor's house, little fights

That will resolve themselves in blood
Unshed, a few silent meals and grace as random
As tomorrow. Write down how men solve problems

The moon for all its height has never seen
And the old gods used to solve by thunderbolts.
The little bones of sleeping bears

Grow strong inside the snow.
Children believe the snow's only fault
Is that when it goes it stays away too long

It is the mystery and myth of man that the moon
returns us to. The greatest grace is to forgive,
as trees forgive the dry days and garden

Birds forgive the hawking wind. The best place
To live is where the world changes like the moon
from week to week and the little bones of bears

grow strong inside their fear. Gods only solve
what they want to, come sunshine or moon gloom.
We watch the waxing moon in its full becoming,

And take our hints from children
who pray that as their parents wane, they
will surely come, like moons, again to bloom.

Garden flowers

He is old now, stooped
as a willow branch from gravity
and the pleasures of cultivation,
the kinds of pleasure a country man
can bear, leaning down to nurture
flowers of broccoli, rows of wax beans,
the convoluted vines that hide tomatoes
from the birds and too much sun,
the humble homes of russet potatoes.

He can't see so well these days. The one eye
tricks him when he isn't looking, turns
things double then doubles again. He spends
each weekday morning picking the ready ones,
gifts he has offered his wife so many seasons
he has forgot are gifts although each time
he feels content, numbering his find,
one for his oldest daughter in Baltimore
one for the one who never lived then died
one for the littlest one grown now and gone
the biggest for his wife of sixty years

When he is ready, this day the asparagi bunched
in one hand, the latest fruit of narrowing rows,
he brings them like flowers to the kitchen door.
She takes them thinking of all the canning ahead,
that she is getting too old for a girl's work,
tells him to wash his hands and sit to table,
the oatmeal is getting cold, he needs his grits.

Blue Jays in the Garden

You and I can name traits we despise
of the blue jay gang: they steal the eggs
Of other nests, are entirely too beautiful, boastful,
Pushy and arrogant at the common feeders, scare off
The sparrows, terrify the cardinals. The doves
Are smart enough to stay away until the jays have left.
But dove eggs have no arms to prevent
The raiding of nests the parents have cunningly built.

It's hard to see the blue jay's beauty for its arrogance
And bullying but even blue jays have their uses.
My friend tells me that his father had a practice
Of shooting one blue jay each planting season
And hanging its feathers near the feed station to scare
The blue jay flock away from the seed put out
for the chickadees and tits. Forty years ago, this was.

Once, he combed through the crop of that year's jay
And discovered a handful of tent caterpillars,
Worms who make of their lives a singular quest
To build their tent in the wild cherry and apple trees.
Many caterpillars die on the way through exhaustion,
By felonious assault or gruesome accident.
But if the blue jays, rapacious feeders, didn't fly
In Connecticut, the State would be tented over
With worm birthing places, all sheer gossamer
And baby worms, netting the autumn trees.

Tent caterpillars are not beautiful, as we know,
They take their meals and treats
And build their houses in trees we love
And can ruin them for man and bird alike.
We shall not deal with why such beasts exist,
The point to allow is that blue jays have
Their purposes: and we've heard they die
Like the rest of us, which solves the pride they are.
But not too soon, Lord of Infinite Design,
We pray for them and us, not too soon.

Farm in Indiana, 1934

A lame-legged blackbird pecked anyway
at our autumn ground. It was the first
time since Easter I heard the sky laugh.

A quiet little chuckle came like rain
from the grove of elderberry on the hill.
Oh I'd seen a smile, as had my father.

That bird's wings weren't broken down.
The air was willing to support him.
My guess is he forgot that he could fly.

There's nothing funny in this universe.
That blackbird limped around and pecked
until even the worms, though they feared,

did not respect him as something far beyond
them, who could lift them into the air
and take them places deeper than hooks.

And then the sky laughed again and the bird
lifted off as natural as moonrise, and flew
at a right angle to the trees, something

I had sometimes dreamed of doing,
toward the town where children laughed
like lollipops and trains moved like eagles
through hills and over rivers, silver streaks.

A Silence of Frogs

Surely there should be some frogs,
The calling croak that says *we are*,
But here there is only silence
Painted into a shallow pond,
Apparently like other ponds
Save that this one is Monet's
And Monet knew
You don't need frogs to fill a pond,
Water lilies will draw the silence in
And make it worth a listening.

An intervening wall saves the space
From being overwhelmed by gossip
Though the guards greet each other
In kind voices suggesting a fear of frog
Ghosts floating with the mist above
The lily pads, carrying their soundings
Of past and future in authentic voices.

Night Trees

We name night's trees to hold away what scares us
As our oldest ancestors did the oldest vengeful gods.
We call them what we recognize against April's sky:
Our memories sharpened by fear of crucifixion.

Crooked old lady with frog, we pray
Brer rabbit kissing Tiny Tim,
Stork on one leg stalking fish.
The wind touches the stand of trees
Just enough we change our minds, say
Moses with tablets, say *Mother weeping, with child,*
Declare epiphanies.

Huddled more closely together under roof.
Although we study, we cannot count the stars.
One planet, disguised as plane, crawls along
Without our naming, her sharp dots dart cargo here
And away, signifying progress, denoting light.

In the morning, we are our separate selves,
Determine everything is hokey dokey in our world,
That the cats have not been eaten by raccoons
The refrigerator not emptied of its treasures.
The scraggled trees are only trees, not ancient aches

And staggered words. The wind softs down
From the eastern hills and it is nearly time
To go to work, to school, to comfort other men
That what they'd seen last night they hadn't seen
And that the path we're on is where we mean to go.

The Way the Wind Blows

Never plant a garden, my neighbor said,
When the wind is blowing northeast.

Now, since a boy, I've never known
Exactly which way the wind is blowing

Man says we've got a southwest wind
Today, I can't get it straight in my mind

Is the wind coming or going and is that what they mean
When they say to my Pa, that lunk of yours don't know

Which side of the door is out and which is in
And my Pa says to them it don't matter a darn,

That boy's bound and determined he'll be a college man
And don't need to know when it's time to remove his thumb

From the hammer descending upon it at a hurtful speed,
Don't need to know and that is that. Boy's smart

Enough, when the wind brings rain, to get under the shed
Or above depending on where he wants to go.

Not that I mind, mind you, taking advice
From them that knows which way the wind blows

But the boy, the boy doesn't care who knows what,
When it's time to go, he'll stay and that is that.

Thoroughbred

The word on the street is Noblest of Nags.
      A long shot worth the gamble, She's game
            In any weather. I'd rather bet a horse like her

Than prima donnas who get scratched from a race
      For nothing much, for nothing at all, a whim
            By a wimp of a trainer. Seems to me a horse

Like Noblest Nag's the kind I'd like
      To have had I the stuff to have a horse
            To show after she's run her share of stakes.

I'd put her in a place of mellow meadows
      Where she could laze away the day and dream
            Of catching Charismatic in the stretch

That Derby Day in '99. Sometimes
      I wonder how for hours they can stand
            In horsely harmony. I'd bet

Old Nag sends many manly lines
      Of Shakespeare's sonnets to her friend, the beat
            Reminding them of races they had run

Or would have. I'd like to stand some day with her
      And hear her heart, the way it sings, and listen
            To the world the way she does, and learn a little how
                To let the world surround me, when I've run enough.

Pineapple

For Rod Jellema

Eating a pineapple in Clodsyvich
I imagined for a moment this was hell,
A fruit in my hand that threatened extinction,
Its knobs and knurls guarding what some god
Who didn't love man overmuch meant us
To take for sweet, for sustenance
Enough a man could climb a tree and look
Seaward toward another time and place,
Hid inside a fruit made for devils and their ilk.

And this, you won't forget, was Clodsyvich,
A town favored by dust devils and a witch
Who had forgotten the spell she needed
To get her gone. One time I sent a friend
A poem from Clodsyvich. She said the words
Dribbled like loose dirt off the page into her soup
And would I not send any others until I moved.
I was so moved I bit right through the hide
Of the only pineapple in the state.

The yellow taste dribbled through
My broken teeth. Now my words slide through the trap
I used to have to keep my tongue in my mouth,
Replacing assonance for consonance and that is why
Clodsyvich no longer lives in my maps of the world
And why that bomb of a fruit is the only one I hate.

GALLERY I

Creatures

Chicken à la Klimt, 34" x 29", acrylic and goldleaf on canvas

Turtle Abstract, 40" x 32", acrylic on canvas

Beta in Red, 15" x 13", acrylic on panel

Frogs, 26" x 23", acrylic on panel

Beta in Blue, 15" x 13", acrylic on panel

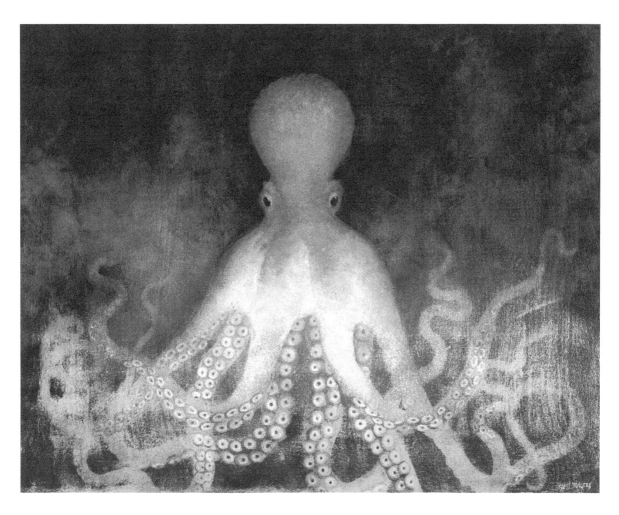

Octopus, 28" x 36", acrylic on panel

Deep Sea Treasures, 40" x 35", acrylic on canvas

Blizard, 39" x 28", acrylic on canvas

Butterflies in Yellow, 29" x 27", acrylic on panel

Brown Chicken, 27" x 29", acrylic on panel

Canary Row, 34" x 39", watercolor on canvas

Clownfish, 30" x 30", acrylic on panel

Discus Fish, 23" x 26", acrylic on panel

Peacock, 36" x 24", ink and acrylic on panel

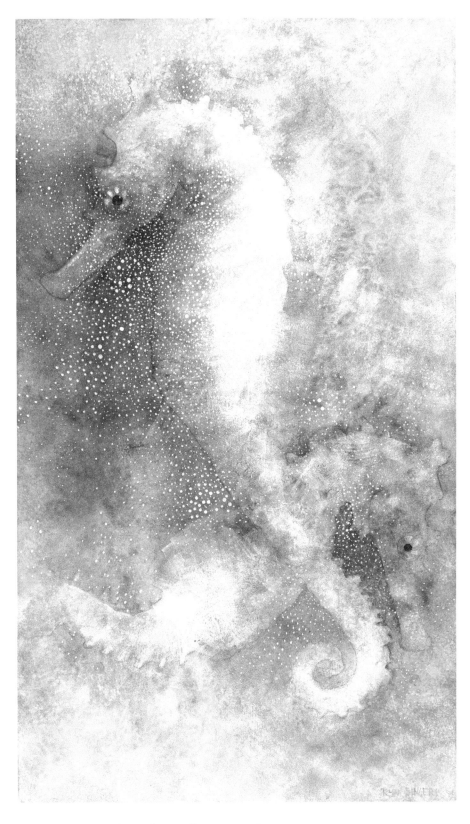

Seahorses, 27" x 16", acrylic on panel

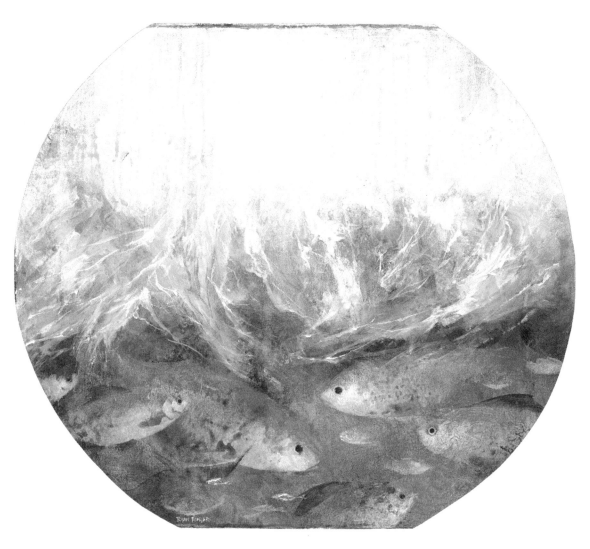

Sea Bowl, 26" x 29", acrylic on panel

Fanta Sea, 39" x 28", acrylic on canvas

Fish 2 Fish, 22" x 23", acrylic on panel

Eye Level, 39" x 39", acrylic on canvas

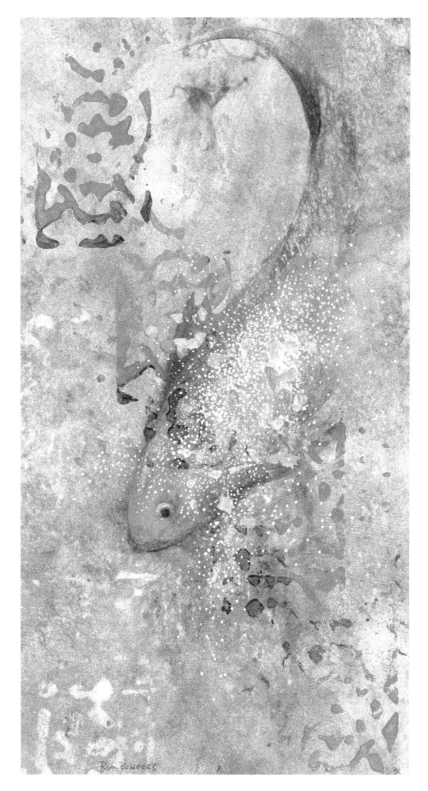

Fish Deco Blu, 17" x 9", watercolor on paper

Goldfish in Blue, 19" x 19", acrylic on panel

Grenn & Berrit, 39" x 27", watercolor and acrylic on canvas

Hidden Angelfish, 22" x 18", watercolor on paper

Humming, 12" x 26", watercolor and acrylic on canvas

Swimming II, 34" x 17", watercolor on panel

Fish in Blue, 26" x 29", acrylic on panel

Swimming I, 34" x 17", watercolor on panel

Lionfish, 34" x 31", watercolor and acrylic on paper

Angelfish, 19" x 19", acrylic on panel

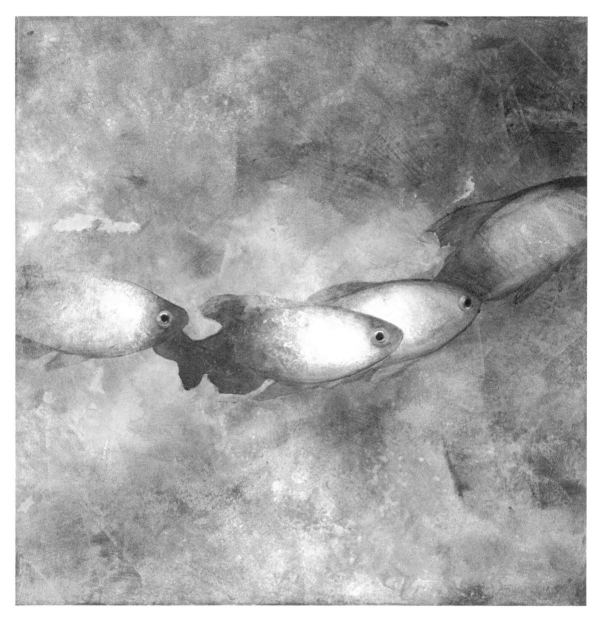

White Fish on Blue, 19" x 19", acrylic on panel

Selections from:

from ***Sounding the Atlantic***
2010

Clown Face

Easter Monday, calendar-wise, the clown
who plies his trade in the circus parade,
whose face grew up from crowded shoulders
in a public place, declares he has had enough
of scaring little children, will put away
forever the paints that name him clown.

The crooked old woman who depends so
on him could not have been less pleased,
nor is the Master clown, who has made
for him allowances, granted benefits
and named him driver of the clown mobile.
They love him for themselves, for his face
in which they see a terror they can share.

Listen yourself and you will hear
the old woman worry the rocking chair.
You too may wonder at the clown's turn
away from the danger of laughter,
and how a man who does so well what he does
can hope to find another way to make a living,
and so deny to children the tightrope of fear
they need a little more than they want joy.

Passive Aggressive

A fifteen-year-old girl speaks

It's like I just like have to kiss
a boy in every city where I am like at.
Its just so totally like I do this. Kiss.
So I am like last year? in Florence?
Italy? So weird.

I mean totally it was like so weird
I hadn't like kissed like one of them?
And I was so totally like bummed.

So I see this really like old man
at the airport and like it's what
I do so I go totally up to him and like
kiss him and it was totally like weird.

He was like twenty-seven and his wife—
it was like Like. She was so
passive aggressive. Like sulked.

I was just like. It was like I did it?
Like totally kept my kiss list going? Weird.

Leaf Raker

She gathers up what nature's left for us
because our houses touch on hers.

Thin as a broom, she sweeps whatever falls
almost as well as the wind, intent on giving shape

to what is left of autumn. Every year
it works. When winter wakes us to surprise

and weathers in our street, she shovels off
the snow covering up those tracks that lead

to us. We call her the quixotress of trees,
mistress of drifts, as if we could shrug off

the way she puts the neighborhood to rights.
Without our leave, she works against the clock

to shape a street that otherwise would fail
to find itself beneath the swarm of falls.

Spring and summer both, she sprinkles seed to meet
the rain. She plugs the ground around our trees

with fertilizers, waits for the magic to happen
to maple, oak and elm, then she gathers up

her autumn tools and sets to work. While she rakes,
she praises the sky for seasons, us for being here.

Marathoner

He hammered his heart until it was ready,
smeared some ointment where it was meant
to be and where it wasn't, laved it on his breath,

his child's favorite soap pipe, his eyes, his teeth,
the belly he'd sooner not have, the spooned meat
for the dog that had to come with him.

He flexed the bald soles of his bottommost bones,
his toes curling in as though afraid
of what was coming, then accepting the burden.

He did the required elongations, the rotations
his training manual forgot, readied his suspensions
of disbelief at what he was about to do,

steeled his eye and the muscles he could reach,
said his kneeldown prayers and fare-thee-wells
and set off, as if a gun had told him, Go.

Harley Rider at Rehoboth Beach

I try to read the scars he wears as map
enough to tell me where he has been.

What's broken in me doesn't like
the tattoos that he has stitched into his chest,

just above the nipples. *Born to Die*, one boasts,
the other *Hell Hound*. That night, she whispers

nothings in my ear of how it feels
to sleep with a hell hound born to die.

Next day, I stand beside him in the surf,
trading stories of other Mains, a storm

that lasted days and finally tossed us up,
the way a Harley can hurt a man.

Office Visit

There's one thing many doctors hate enough to say.
Ask yours about his own preoccupying pain.

If you promise to pay, he will tell you that it's pure
and as fragile as a spinster aunt, grown poor

and speckled gray with ancient losses.
My psychiatrist protests that there is less

to his problem than he wanted. He would rather
every habit would be worse than his father's.

How the smell of his nurse curls into his hair
makes my bone man shave his arms and wish her

Ivory clean. He tells me his wife has a passion
for manifest pistils and manifold stamens

and makes him poison that that would kill her blooms.
When she hears her knife-hand knuckles creak,

my surgeon thinks of vises and the cracking
voice she has and means to lose. The radiologist

has a smile tucked inside her dimple, detests
the multiplying malignant cells of men.

My neurologist tells me only what is certain:
the two of us will go to many doctors in our time.

He hopes I have the craft to mute my rage
and the art to suffer all of theirs with grace.

Still Life Study

An apprentice to the craft could draw
You, perfect squirrel, in motion,
your belly slung low in a physics right
for one of your size and disposition.
It's plain the tree was your retreat
In the hawk-lit woods, your helmeted head
Poised to see threats coming
Peripherals keened by art beyond ours.

How right to be a squirrel in such a place,
your face as full of pleasure as the nut
filling the shell. What prodigious leaps,
what sheers of will, flinging yourself
from done branch to undone. Still, in the tree-
less world you run a fatal risk. Tires
blind and straight as crutches don't go for craft,
your fake left, go left. They round their lives
in a minor league, leave you a question mark.
No skill to that sport, nothing worth your move

of his book named Photographs in gold.
Museums, cathedrals, the Capitol,
all frozen fragments of the public city
safely at rest, safely white on blue.
One time he took a picture by mistake,
an old man staring at the lens
from three feet out. He hides this one
away, ashamed of the out-of-focus eyes,
the deep lines a bit more distance
would disguise. He pencils in a note
to find out more about his field of vision.
This man shoots to kill a little time.

Cream

She likes to remember the cows
for the steam that rises from them
autumn and spring as if their mouths
were all of them, as if their bodies
were locomotives, starting up again,
as if they were the earth itself,
rising into clouds, becoming rain,
machines, as clean and right as when
machines were new and quiet in the world,
knew when to move and when to rest,
spent much of their being waiting to be,
the dumb power a gentle hum on the earth,
making a name by simply being there.

She likes to think of them as sisters
to her, lying down, half-drowsed
in pasture, ready to be something else,
and rising together to walk with her
into the houses of men, another life.

She sees them now, their large heads
placid and heavy on their settled bodies,
grouped under a tree as if for a painting,
their browns and whites blending into the soft
shades of spring the painter has made for them
and moves herself as in a dream of cow,
across the fence, across the meadow.
She means to lie down in their midst,
the hot flanks breathing on her skin,
and go to sleep. When she wakes, her face
will be licked clean and in her hands
the warm teats will swell and gush.
She will wash like the queen of hearts in cream.

Heron Bay

There is a space for winter here
To grow its ice. There is a place
For a small boat with oars and sail.
There is a piece of water here
For a fish farmer and his old wife,
Turned by the wind into the wind.
We say the night heron stands and waits
For breaking water. He knows that water yields,
That fishes break. His neck is a white slake
Fishing for the water's sake and his.
He takes only his place which is as small
As he needs. He leaves the rest to you
And me, a small boat, winter and a pair
Of old crabbers leaning into the wind,
Space for oceans to turn in, things that bend.

Soundings Near the Atlantic

The man of many trousers is no fool, pulls over
for the Rescue Squad's red blare that means what it says.
He is still and stopped in the kind of groove
he hoped he had left in the city, at work, away
from this corn and chicken town two miles west
of the easy rock and roll of the breaking Atlantic.

A carload of outraged music and teenage boys
trails in the wake of the ambulance, their radio
speaking decibels for them about the mess it is
being a teenage boy, the sounds they know
are coming before they give themselves away.

He has been granted the ear to think that the crickets
in his pear tree make as much noise as horny boys,
and for the same basic reasons. The last time
he was surprised by sound, a girl with hair as long
as winter breath had come up behind and passed

him on the boardwalk, her bare feet whispering
threats different and more serious than the slap
and pause slap and pause of his loose sandals.
A man of sungrown freckles takes the morning kite
to air to get a feel for what the weather promises.

for his shored kids, reeling the string with slow regard
for the gulls, that he not strangle one by accident
and add too early to the shore's run of scalloped edges.
He has heard his daughter lecture even God about the care
of living things and he, decidedly this morning, is not He.

The locals have a word or two for us, the walkers on their sand,
the crowded talkers on the boardwalk they alone have wintered,
they and the skittering gulls and the lapping sea. The chicken skinners
teach their kids the language that they use to get the city folk into focus.
The kids have a language of their own—for us and for their parents both.

The oldest men mumble in their sleep soft prayers they learned
when silence circled the country fields like chicken hawks.
When she is called to speak at the PTA, a daughter of the town
conplains about the new teacher who has come from Baltimore
and never been to church one time. The babies don't have the words

yet but their tongues itch to get at the bitter home-made cider.
Near the bearding corn, the wings of a hummingbird wind up
To such a pitch that a dragonfly squadron start their engines.
The Atlantic feathers the beach with whispers from the East.
Something older than gossip is about to be heard.

Weekday Morning

For Steve Knox b. 10/10/1910 – d. 10/10/2006

He measures his walk, stooped
as a willow branch from gravity
and the pulls of cultivation,
the kinds of pleasure a country man
can bear, leaning down to nurture
flowers of broccoli, rows of waxbeans,
the convoluted vines that hide tomatoes
from the birds and too much sun,
mounding the homes of russet potatoes.

He can't see so well. The one eye
tricks him when he isn't looking, turns
things double. He takes his time
a weekday morning picking cucumbers
and carrots, numbering his find,
  a gather for his oldest daughter in Baltimore,
  and one for the baby who never quite grew up,
  the biggest for his wife of sixty-six years.

When he is ready, the new pick bunched
in one hand, the latest fruit of narrowing rows,
he brings them like flowers to the kitchen door.
She takes them thinking of the canning ahead,
that she is getting slow for a girl's work,
tells him to wash his hands and sit to table,
the eggs are getting cold, he needs his grits.

Trapeze Artist Under the Big Top

Fellina the Falling Star
performs her life-defying swoops
and swings above the center ring.

Gainers, Double Gainers, Jack-
Knives, Flips, she does them all,
finds momentum in the letting go,

remembers one time one platform
next time the other, the view toward
a farther side beyond what we can see.

And in between, the slippery bar awaits her,
like yours and mine who every time
hold on to nothing more than air.

She recovers on the backward swing
and sometimes on the downward rush
exults with a joy that we can fathom.

Nothing is guaranteed under the Big Top,
only the momentary stop,
the catching on beyond the letting go.

Blind Girl

If you've not run your face into a wall,
I've never spit a gun at birds
                or hit a deer

before its chance to move into the mottle
and I can tell the truth of deeper blue
better than you can ever shout
                of red that awful red

While I've not seen your shapes and sizes,
you have not plumbed the depths of black
I have behind my eyes, the ways
they talk and walk me through the steps
                I need and want to dance.

Describe for me the color of clean.
I'll tell you how a scrubbing feels inside.
And when you see the conductor raise his stick,
I'll tell you how the hidden drums will march
                to wake the sleepy violins.

Baloney Sandwiches

The night fiend with the pale blue complexion
Lived under my bed when I was nine
And old enough to dress for church and multiply
by nines. He reminded me of sour milk.
I did not fear him, I feared his smell
And how I used to gag on Monday mornings
When I drink cod liver oil. My sister watched,
her pigtails like a metronome of No.

I'd talk to him despite the smell sometimes,
Recounting my grievances against cruel fate
And an old aunt who smelled like mustard.
Once I invited him to show himself and fight.
He said *I'm the night fiend, Dope*, and went to sleep.
Did I say he sharpened his nails on the springs
And sang to himself the old ghoul songs?

I was a terrible lot of a lad
My best friend popped me in the nose
Because he talked like brakes
were in his throat and I laughed.
Roses grow best in chicken poop
My mother said. Imagine that. Poop.
The night fiend went into the army when
I turned ten. Good thing, too.
This growing up took all my wits.

Teacher's Pet

"My Johnny ain't no rose. Learn him. Don't smell him."
                                            –Parent to teacher at PTA, 1898

These mountain women. Come in here, I swear,
Like wild goats and tell us how to teach their kids.

The men are just as bad, grunting and belching
Straight through my preparation. The pigs.

I'd like to see that mother try to show a strapping boy
How to find the hypotenuse of a triangle,

Lean down to him and guide his hand
When he stinks like a stuck toilet, nothing less.

I'd just like to see her. And the father too
Though what I heard, he has gone to the city

These two months past, taking his own smell
With him and good riddance.   Maybe I can do

What's right by holding Roddy back. Teach him how
To speak himself right clear and practice pen-

Manship. It's more than that mother will do,
For sure. And besides, he's big enough

To shoe a horse. It's about time he learned
There's other ways a woman can be

Than her ill-favored ways. I swear to cheese
Her Roddy is a boy worth keeping on

Through harvest time. At least by then he's grown
and ready for those wagons coming down the road.

Screened Bird

A curious bird invaded our vacant space
This early spring, made the usual mockery
Of the screen door's need to keep
The outside out, slipped through and killed
Herself for the vision that she had.

No harm in that except the summer porch
Meant for sitting in and looking out
Became her slaughter house. Another bird
I almost met a couple of years ago
Died in our attic, battered by studs,

Pierced by rooting nails, surrounded
by the hard and dark with nothing to drink
But mouse droppings, nothing to eat
But silverfish. Expected death. Okey-dokey,
A way to go where he had to anyway. But to live

Like this other one for weeks inside a place
Where light is all around, the walls soft lies,
Is close enough to our brief passings-by you'd think
I'd sympathize, find common ground
With Icarus and this dark starling. I don't.

I use the iron shovel for her bier, to dig the hole,
For the distance that I have been told to keep
Her germs away from mine, from such a cleaning
Up that might mean death inside and out. I sweep
The feathers into a pile for the kids to understand
The corner where we found her, I teach right angles,

Newton's Laws. The crescent left in the screen as record
Of her passing through and how and where has been
Repaired. We're safe enough from bugs to sit out now.
All summer long, I read the dropping sky for songs
But nothing comes except some show off storms.
Now and then in sleep or half awake, I hear her flap
Of fury against the attic floor and know that dreams
Are stirring up the joys of being blind, with wings.

Coblentz's Farm

It's as good a way as any to plant
A farm against the rolling hills
Of Frederick County. Just get
A herd of milking cows to hold
The meadow down and a Boss cow, bold
Enough to stand alone, to show them how
To find their way to the milking shed
And the farmer's mothering hands.

Bluewash the fence that's only there
To keep the cows content and let
The long arm of the road bend in comfort
around the hickory trees and toward the house
That hides itself behind the barns.

While you're at the painting chore, you might
As well bluewash the roofs of the buildings too,
As soft reminders of the sky that's home
To traveling clouds. The cows will tell you how
To measure the hours before each night.
The deepening blue will tell you of the years.

If I were you I'd get myself an artist man,
Pay him a bucket of milk warm from the teats
To put the softness of the farm in solid terms.
He will know to let the cowgate burn a little red,
To have the shade fall like tongues toward the cows
And lick the meadow to a coolness after noon sun.

So the neighbors can see how things are on your farm,
I'd have him paint that Boss cow red and white
To shine like a beacon, and shape a fence
That's meant to keep nobody in or out
Unless it happens you're a cow. I'd tell him last
To let the road broaden its welcome as it ends,
To let the canvas dress the walls of memory
And lead us back who have been long away.

Parting the Air

You swallow chewing gum, the mother says,
Your blood and bones will bunch together
The kidneys lock in what it should let out,
The stomach stick to the pancreas. You'll clog

Your joints so tight you can't make a move
Especially on the court when you want to fake
Left go left, have to stand where you are
Till you aren't. What the father says:

You swallow a watermelon seed, that's it,
Like an unmilked udder, like your brother's balloon,
Bigger and bigger until you're about to burst
And you will. You're a cat, you swallow grass,

You've seen what happened to our calico. Like that.
You swallow someone's line, you're a flopped fish,
You're a bird with a tooth-ache instead of a fish,
you're hooked, done for. You'd be better off to bite

Your own tongue before you do that, eat your good shirt,
Swallow your words before you do that.
Let me ask you this: you ever see a swallow fly
Above a field of young chewing gum?

He keeps going, right? Would not stop for a Wrigley's
Even if you gave it to him free for nothing. Smart,
That bird, eating his flies on the fly,
Making his way from here to there, parting the air.

Army Sawbones

We remove a lot of limbs in all the seasons.
The taking down has its own reasons

as compelling as the putting up, more studied too,
more art than science will accept, than craft construe,

this swift cut through the bone, tying off the trunk,
splicing roots together, lowering the hunk

of dead limb to the ground. It used to be that Spring
was slow. Few things break then, the sap sings

in limber boys. Here's one now. When he fell,
his taking down was carried off so well

the nerves won't sense for months the leg is gone.
They pulse useless to a brain knows the knuckled bone

will calce with its own boot the footless stump.
Those antique butchers, snow and freezing rain, we lump

with modern pains like napalm, hand grenades. We cut true
no matter what the cause. We are the civilizers, screw

the old bone to the new, synthetic shape, meld
the joint, send the soldered soldier home to mend.

Now the taking down owns all the seasons.
We saw limbs. All men own the reasons.

Antietam's Bloody Lane

The old woman from County Cork keens
For her sons who fell and broke
In a foreign place called Bloody Lane,
Boy-yos who died in blood mud in Maryland
And will not be waked in their mother's parlor
Nor have the priest say the *Sanctus Sanctus*
Sanctus for their wedding Masses.

Some of the women will allow themselves anyway
To believe the Irish boys still live, have gone west
To gold and glory. Soon enough,
They promise the lads will send for them.
Soon enough, they will all be together
In Chicago, in Philadelphia, those odd
Sounding pieces of heaven.

Bloody Lane, men of too much mercy named it.
Bloody it is, and a wretched fine place for a brawl.
Picked at and primped as you never were
In life for your Wake, you get your ride
To a grave in the forgetting ground, the dry
Cold ground the Never Ending Ladies will keep
To work off days of Purgatory.

Better to fight with the other lads for a cause
You'd an inkling of and nothing more.
Better to go, as the Union Sergeant said,
Where you would be safe from Chicago's cold
And a bed as empty as the English heart.

Bloody it is, the lane in Antietam,
And dark enough you could find
Your soul if you're looking to.
The sons of the sons of your uncles' sons
Will play the pipes of an evening for Bloody Lane
And for Gettysburg and for the end of you, you lads
Of County Cork and Kerry and old Mayo.

After the Battle at Seven Pines

Sometimes, after the guns had stilled,
We would hear a girl laugh, the sound
As strange as frogs in the flour bin.
Those two days at Seven Pines,
It seemed as if we forgot how to smile.

Smiling, I figured, was a foreign thing
That needed muscles I didn't have,
All of mine having gone to hiding out,
Ducking down, sliding through mud
That grabbed me with a hundred hands.

I'd like to meet the man from North or South
Could laugh and mean it after Seven Pines.
Fair Oaks, some folks call it, but that was later.
He'd have a different place to stand than mine,
Or be a little mad, which I could understand.

The Man with the Hoe at the Getty Museum

Jean-Francois Millet, 1862

Except for the sackcloth blouses
His wife has stitched together
From the gut of last year's cow,

Except for a club he leans on
To keep him almost vertical
Who otherwise would fall
Down into a spiral of hardscrabble
Except for the thick peasant shoes
That fan out like cudgels, like art,

Except for the wisps of smoke
Behind him, rising to blend
With the gray blue sky of LA,
Except for his eyes that now and then
Saw something as well and clearly
As man could and could name it
Before it went away,

Except for Millet, except for Millet
The tourist who passes, scratching his arms
In wonder in the way of immigrants
To a rich country, scratching his behind
To stir deadened blood and fat
To join the working brain,

Except for Millet, the man from the customized bus
Would never, nor could he, name
What he saw, what he for a moment became.

The Burghers of Calais

I

Rodin's burghers in the sun
are no less men than when
they stood in mud or snow.
Their faces are more fluid, sure.
Bronze glints off the foreheads.

One neck, exposed and bent,
glistens in the afternoon,
but changed? No, not at all,
not utterly, not the way
they changed in Calais.

Two look straight on, but down,
not willing anymore to meet
the little pity of passers-by.
One turns as if to speak against
his shoulder, maybe to the man

behind, who turns himself away.
His arms are dropped weights
that will not ever rise again.
His empty palms face out
the way a child's will

when he has nothing left
against the father's rage.
To his left, a fifth man throws
his right arm up as if to block
a blow, his left side staggers.

He sags above a key he holds,
too heavy for an earthly thing.
The last man bows his head into
both hands and, standing, starts
a fall that will not stop.

II

In Spring, the Burghers
lose their way no less
than fall, are almost warm
enough to loosen up.

They won't though, not now,
not when Rodin has stopped
them cold and left them there,
almost leaning on each other.

In winter, they don't put on
their overcoats, don't shiver
at the sky. Summer's always been
their season, when they shine.

III

They're set almost by chance. In Washington
we often take directions by their stance,
caught like them between Capitol and monument.
Two, almost beside each other, straighten
toward the north. To their east, there's one
who turns as if to make one final plea toward

what follows him. The southern figure looks
north and west. The one who's mostly lost
looks out in what is not a mock despair.
There's one of them who holds his head
in both hands and his eyes on the ground
which is only fixed as long as you look.

IV

They stand there still. Look closer,
there's not a one of them but moves.
Like time, they stand there, like stone.

In the middle, a puddle forms, a
water glazed as they. Though we've
had sun all day, it lasts till dusk,

caught in that little place
at the dead center of the six
who remain the burghers of Calais

though a hundred years have passed
since they've been thrown together
and bid, Be still, Be still..

The Egg Man in Warsaw

After Z. Beksinski's No. 26

Having painted what he could only see
Through fingers sharpened on the wheel of war
Turned in a city he would leave as men must,
He went home to eat for man must eat
And lay with his wife in a feather bed

      For man must pretend to sleep in the end.
      Body to body they lay and prayed that death
      When it came would take away their bones
      With their skin, with their will always to eat
      And procreate, always to make dreams

Out of the emptied city. Bombed emptied squares
Stared where his parents used to meet their friends
For some quiet talk. What he found to draw
Was the perfect shape that is an egg, A head
In blacks and whites and blood of a man

      Of bones making his way across the city.
      Now this is the nightmare, he thought,
      For he knows that an egg is not a predator
      Though arms and legs grow from it,
      He knows that the egg is his Polish neighbor

And that the blood egg of his neighbor's face,
Swathed in impermanent hospital gauze,
Couldn't be, couldn't ever be more than it is,
And when he awoke, as he had to, he went
Directly to Wenceslaw Square and there it was

      Walking like any old nightmare, bones crouched
      For good or ill, and not at all ashamed to be seen so,
      The egg being where he started from, rich fruit
      Of rich thighs given to peace, thighs offered in love.
      Overhead, birds flew, who did not want to be included.

Artisan

A man whose only left arm
has been stroked by his brain
into a stillness beyond his power
to command or change and hangs still,
waiting for what will and will not come,
this man, this stroked man,
is helping his young son dig a hole
in the sand, using his feet as hands,
his legs as arms. The man's an artisan,
shaping what the boy knows
will swallow the ocean.

With clenched toes, the man
routes for them a quick escape
in case the water thinks to do
what water may. He knows the way
a little flooding here and there can hurt
a summer hole beyond redemption,

Though if they have to start again
from scratch, with buckets and tools,
his son will remember
what sand has never thought
and teach the artisan anew how to put
aside what has been done
and find his happiness in absences.

Guernica at the Museum

We concede to the painting we have before us
that soon we will tire even of this lucidity
and need to walk in the sun of the Mall.
The rockets, we are told, face toward Silver Spring
And Fairfax. Inside the cone, we are safe.

Guernica is clean and free from random writing.
The frame does not intrude on what is art.
True, The figures weird the eye.
Is there something to be remembered here?
Whatever shall we do with what we see?

Our guide says to bring the eye in closer,
To notice the colors, how they bulk and smear.
Better, he says, to notice that
than what is being thought,
Better still to walk into the sun while you can.

The gun-ships circle our public places
like beneficent birds They would never fire
where we are, we are assured by public faces,
Can go back to the gallery to study beauty
Wrought from common things, a small girl at a fence,
a field of flowers here, pieces of dead men there.

Practicing the Art in New Jersey

"The profound change has come upon them"
                    —W.C. Williams

You, baby doctor,
pulling boys out
by their toes, finding two
or three baby girls up your sleeve
by legerdemain, getting
it all down to a science,
I hear you have plumbed
a couple of poems
the other morning, put
them down on the pad
you use to prescribe
the medicines we need.

That's an artful thing
to do, making changes
that matter, getting them
underway the way
you've been taught,
giving us all a chance
we would not have had
without that little tug
toward a change that you,
you baby doctor, prescribed
in your hot medicinal scrawl.

Tehran Hod Carrier

Doubled up for good and all, a turn
he has been taught by an excess of brick,
and a deficiency of calcium in the bones,

the Persian hod-man, with a mother
who has worn a sari all her days and nights,
even in bed, even at the moment of his conception,

and a wife who wears high heels and walks
a toy dog to prove she is a modern woman
and proud of the life she has stitched together.

The hod man has—even bent to brick—
a common sense not to show a mean obeisance
to mullahs or puffy businessmen.

Turned earthward as he is, he has trained himself
to focus as few of us have chance or pleasure
on the industry and the friendly ways of ants,

He is long past straightening out. He does
What he does, taught by ants and saints,
Despite the emptying stares of the money men

who require only to be obeyed, with only the ladder rungs
curled to hold him, and as he climbs he will sing
for reasons I can not—though I have tried—construe.

Spider Webs

The girl who loved spider webs
Had much to mull with herself.

She wondered at the two strands
Of anchoring the spider makes

And why she smelled rock when she saw
A web grow between the sliced hills.

Before she knew about the boys,
Their stone-sure hearts,

Their spinning hands, she tried
Her skill at weaving a spider-web

But couldn't get the knack so turned
At last to soccer in the far field.

Rocky-thin and safe from mountains
And smart enough to shelter from thunder,

She would kick the ball to herself
At the other end, then run like a boy

Had never done and kick it back again.
In the early morning, the webs would work

At gathering the mist and pretending
That their design was beauty, nothing more.

Some flies got fooled, but she never did,
Not once in all the years she kicked that ball

And ran after it. After those apprenticeships,
She studied mountains for their art and brought

A man to herself who knew to kick a ball as hard
as she did and could gentle a spider in his hand.

Goat Farming at Flat Rock

Carl Sandburg liked a little honey
in his morning coffee which he never drank
till afternoon, a proper time for a poet to rise
who had been at it half the night.
He took some goat's milk to lighten the cup,
give the coffee a taste worth looking toward.

His wife rose early, raised prize goats from the go,
the get, fed the kids two at a time in the cold kitchen
she'd had built at Connemara, a name they kept
because it fit. In a single year, one of those prize goats
produced forty seven hundred pounds of milk,
a Flat Rock record that may stand as long as goats give milk.

Carl weighed the words he meant to use each week.
They lifted off the scales like bees, would not stay put for anything,
as busy as his language had the need to be
trying to prise itself from traps. He woke late, snuck up on syllables
that swelled like honeyed hives, milked them through the nights
among the rocks, stroked them, honeybee and goat, into the poem.

Beyond the Hot Sun

The old man who lives alone near the sea
can only make things out in certain light,
with eyes that love old men and horizons.
The rest of us will have to learn the grace
of growing, how it is to look beyond the hot
sun, how to let the eye feel the way
toward what it will with luck become.

The old man wraps the scarf of night around him
and lifts it off for morning work. He is content
to do his stretching exercises, limbering up
for the long walk he means to take
before he shakes himself like an old dog,
gives the ocean a drink of his plenitude,
lets himself be seen by us for what he is,
and shrugs for what he isn't anymore.

Weathering the Front Door

Ah. For the deep heaven's sake,
I'm fed up entirely.
Let's have an Irish door, at least,
if we can't have the brawn and the stout
and the smell of peat in the house.

You pick the paint, I'll slap it on,
a cardinal red lacquered sheen
with brass to announce and brass
to let in and the hinges too, brass,
swinging as bold as the money
down the street.

      Remember how we practiced for the wedding
      after the last sun storm of earliest spring
      had sworn off and headed up to Boston.
      Took the door down, we did, the way it went up,
      flipped it flat on the spring onions starting to sprout,
      waxed it so our feet would shine and snap.

To qualify our steps for heaven,
when late spring springs its tricks,
we'll take down the door again and put
our dancing shoes on, the taps of them
beating a jig and a reel into the air, give us
a walking out together above the dirt
like we are more than man and woman.

It's a way of letting the neighbors know
of the merry mischief to come, this taking down
the door. It's a way of letting the feet fly
that would be stuck and held in the mud.
We'll only be taking it down at last to celebrate
the goings-on of those worth going on about:

but when we do we'll drop it right outside
the threshhold so the bride and groom can reel

from the garden path into the house and bed
can hear the young ones tapping up their heels
and toes and us ourselves singing so boisterous loud
the words echo off the ground and the answering sky.
Having occasions it is. Why we have the front doors.

Gravities

Got nose to nose with ants, I did,
to get our signals straight, about our needs.
Came eye to bulged eye with a hungry frog
Thrust beyond himself for living's sake.

When I heard the ways things work,
I tried the boneyard stumble,
letting my whole sack of immortality
and noble thoughts—my serene self itself

come separately to a ground as hard
as pulled triggers on elbow and knee.
Try falling once yourself, astonished man,
as natural as tomorrow, and stagger up

all aches and crinks and joy at having them.
Now, then, to the wobble of wheel, the hill
that means to keep us in our place,
the parachute, the wizardry of rain.

Hilda & Me & Hazel

These stories are as true as clocks
though there are some in this town
think I would make up the goings-on
just so I would have my say.
What we are about is partly underground
and partly overhead, or that what was.

Happens I catch myself a baby mockingbird,
get him right here in this hand closed up,
his whole body shaking like some old
jalopy Ford that needs a tune-up bad,
his tail feathers tickling my palm
like he is a girl wants something that
I got and she don't. I hear that once
it smells of people, the mother won't
have nothing more to do with it,
so I start to pull the feathers off,
one at a time, stacking them up
real careful in a matchbox that I keep
against emergencies like this, figuring if
I catch enough of them this year maybe
I will stuff myself a pillow for my head
and maybe one for Hilda and for Hazel too.
Like any damned fool, which some will say
my mother didn't raise none of, I take
my eyes away from what I am doing for a sec
when wham! that mother mocker's at my eye
pulling like we are playing at a tug of war.
The mother makes toward the middle branch.
I'm off my feet by now, then something snaps
like a whole string of rubberbands has broke
and I am back on the ground where I began.
I only need the one eye anyway, though things
have flattened some, the way I see it now.

The next one, Hilda likes. She says it shows
that fools is fools in uniform or not.

So the story is a fat black snake that curls
around our cellar water tank like it
is desperate ripe in love or similar to that.
The snake will not let go despite
the talking to I give it good, from me
who undisputable do not take to snakes.
So I have to get the police here
to get it gone and the police says
he would have to have my social security
first, the number, before he could go below
the ground floor, says it is a rule.
Finally I give the number up. He goes,
beating his stick on each of the going down
steps, hollering like Calvin by god Coolidge
is the President. The snake by then is gone as gold
but that doesn't stop the police from taking out
his .45 and shooting about two and one-half
holes straight through the hot water heater
plus the one bullet that bounces all around
like Willy Masconi's triple cushion trick
until that bullet finds the furnace wall that spits
out soot and flame enough to set the house to fire.
The local Hose and Ladder Company alarm
themselves to help things out. It's me
could tell them how to put a fire down,
could tell them how to use a shovel too.
Anyhow, the next unwelcome guest that calls,
we make our mind up there and then will best
be dealt with by ourselves, my sisters who
you will hear about and me, who is Henry
that you already know don't take too much
of prompters to tell his side of things.

So this story is the skunk.
My sister Hazel grabs the softball bat.
Hilda, who is the other sister, ankle yanks
her wading boots. We head outside,

me with the bullet gun in the lead and she
and she behind to sight the polecat out for us
because of my flat eye and everything about
the gun. We've had about enough of the skunk
who has put his smell beneath our sitting porch
as if he means to stay and be one of us,
or start a family of his own to add
to the general stink of things. I circle back
toward the front, my gun cradled to my gut,
tipping toe like I was showed. Hazel's 53,
still sets her hair in curlers every day,
turning the hangs around like they was snakes.
Hilda, who is the other, doesn't damned well care
about much of anything except her feet and keeping
them away from that that bites or cuts or stings,
or, as in the present case, that stinks.
My tobacco's caught where it can give
me juice the times I need a shot of it,
especially just before I shoulder up my .22.
take aim. Sister Hazel's curler spikes,
they're green, same as the halter she
puts on—to brighten up the place, she says.
Hilda, the other one, plays the piano accordian
in her boots, two tunes she has learned
by heart and by pecking at the keys
so they're and we're about worn out
from the acculturation.

Skunks is skunks, I say, no matter what.
Happens that Hazel, her with the soft heart
and the bat as mean as her head, starts around
the other side, beating on the ground enough
to wake the dead that are not, quite.
I am talking here about our neighbors to the west,
city folks, the ones I mean to get to next.
Now, here comes this skunk looking almost
too small for his smell, hopping like the fool

and baby rabbit our own mother showed up with
one Easter week and promptly died, as if we cared.
So now the skunk is running toward Hilda's foot,
her with the Sears and Roebuck guaranteed-rubber
knee-high wading boots. I shoot as if I mean to,
leading the skunk the way my uncle Billy taught me.
Same as most other times, I miss.
The bullet skitters like a flat rock
skimming water. Hazel shrieks out loud
like it is somebody she knows been shot.
The gun remembers what it sounds like,
lets the neighbors know that everything is O.K.
and that their skunk, the one they meant to give
away, is coming back across the road from us to them.

After dinner (Hazel sets the extra place
just, she says, in case), we will sit and sort
things out, remember how we always know
to work together, all of us, willynilly,
working like we did, had to, the time
that Hazel had herself a man come calling
that I did not know and did not like
no matter what and I surprised my own self
and them with what I did and did not miss.
The ground we stuck it in beneath the porch
is soft, the smell's near gone for good and all.
No snakes, no skunks, no nothing underground
or overhead that stops us three from getting on.

The thing about the baby mockingbird,
the thing that really gets me is,
the wind came up and all the feathers flew.
Sweet Jesus, I'd have liked to seen them go,
flying on their own, making like they were whole.

Candidate

Here's a man we could elect,
his wonderfully straightforward teeth
dropping toward the carrot,
no doubt at all about his appetite.
His resume, his being itself
is pure American:
the friendly impertinence
of "What's up, Doc?
the democratic urge
to know what's going on.

He dons the gray and white suit
as well as any diplomat,
 reveals a nakedness that says
there's nothing here to hide or fear.
The world's a carrot to old Bugs.
An appetite for our time.
A ready hand for practical jokes,
some slapstick, the legerdemain
to pluck a carrot out of the air,
a stammer that hides the wise man.

The every ready fall guy
is by his side ready to fool,
old Elmer Fudd, but love too,
love for being such a perfect flub
and bald and fat and short. A pal
we all should have. So when old Bugs
says "That's all, folks," with his wink,
we know he means that's all for now,
that we'll see him in the White House
if we only keep our wits about us.

The Purposes of Circuses

I used to know a guy, at least I wish I did
Who could stand on one finger for a minute flat.

I never said he could dance at the same time,
Did I? I never said I really knew him,

But I saw him once at the Greatest Show
On Earth. Saw him true

With these very eyes. I even got to counting down
Or counting up depending on your numbers system

Fifty one, fifty two, like that. And by the end,
I was cheering like raspberries were in season.

I tried it once myself when I was in the Navy
And full of beans. Had a swabbie pal hold my legs

Up toward the stars and said now watch this watch
And broke my middle finger then my nose flat out.

One thing they never teach you about circus tricks:
Actually, a couple things… but then you grow up

And you either know or you don't you were meant
To marry the girl on the flying trapeze or you weren't

And that kids should show off when you're young,
And when they get older, they shouldn't.

GALLERY II

Still Lifes

Lizards, 20" x 16", oil on panel

Bird & Pomegranates, 11" x 16", oil on panel

Barbara's Mice, 20" x 31", oil on canvas

Freeing Red, 20" x 16", oil on panel

Colors 2, 18" x 24", oil on canvas

Dragonflies, 28" x 39", oil on canvas

Lemon Study, 11" x 16", oil on panel

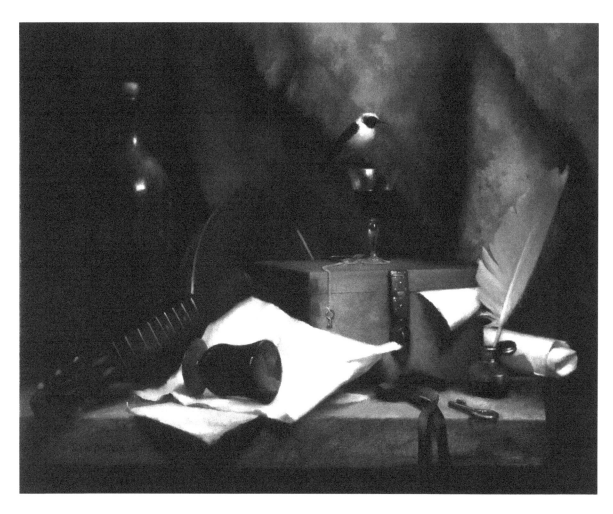

Letters, 24" x 36", oil on canvas

Fruit, 18" x 32", oil on canvas

Riding Gear, 20" x 28", oil on canvas

Still Life, 20" x 30", oil on canvas

Studio Corner, 40" x 28", oil on canvas

The Book, 26" x 19", oil on canvas

Oranges on Bashir, 20" x 16", oil on canvas

from **Wild Card**
1989

Plea to A Vogue Model

To let the rude bones show, and showing, break
the easy flow of form that dulls the eye
lulled by its soft falls. Let the ears protrude
like whelks from a head smooth as damp sand.
to let the shoulder blades, like torn wings, block
the sleek descent of back. To let the elbows
In crazy triangles dance like marionettes
pulled by finger and fling.

The bald knees also know a thing or two
About what is comely rude. And splayed feet,
With bones beyond the fingering, like birds. bones
that never can be mended once they crack,
break paths no architect, for all his flow,
could follow. But small boys could, and mad
old women, bent to shape, and sometimes,
sometimes, when you forget and be glad
of the girl that is awkward in you, you.

Scar

Her mother taught her rudiments of dress,
white gloves and pantaloons, white shoes
for formal teas. In rain, her father made
her wear galoshes shaped like hippopotami
glistening with fat. Her sister told her what

she had to hear: how to put off taking off
the clothes she would learn to wear so well
that certain men would want them for their own
designs, or so they would say. No one showed her
how to wear the scar she found herself when she

was older. She satin-stitched it on from eye to chin.
In her waiting room, she takes off everything she can.
The scar is thrown across a chair. Like the child
that she was, she lies in bed, talking to herself,
with all she is before her and nothing left to learn.

Breaking Eggs at the Cozy Diner

Each morning he comes in for the Trucker's Bite
(two eggs, French toast, a chunk of steak),
looks straight ahead at the kitchen door,
derricks the food toward his mouth, and chews
toward his leaving, belches once or twice
like a diesel truck starting up, quiet but strong,
picks up his check, puts down a two-bit tip,
and motors out to work whatever work
it is he does on all that food.

Every day the waitress who has brought
him all the things he needs, mother more
than mistress in her cups, picks up what
he has left and breaks a couple eggs inside
her apron pocket just to hide the two-bit tip
which every day he drops. She takes away
her dreams like dirty dishes shoved
beneath the front seat of the pick-up truck
he drives to breakfast at the Tastee Diner.

One time she'd like to conjure up what's to
be fried next, as slick as rabbits from her cape.
What she wants more than her appetite is
the utter mastery of one small thing, finesse
the likes of which she's watched on Channel 26.
The sure slide through water of a trout, the way
a willow tree knows how to ride the wind.
Some weekday nights, her hand drips yellow
as she dips to fish the two-bit tip.

Deer Legs in Rappahannock County

The hunters hang their city smells
on the January woods. They shed the hacked-
off limbs of the doe they would rather not
be caught with. The deer's discarded parts
won't nose the place until the April flaw.

From winter's graver yards, the farm dogs
practice old economies. Mouths as patient as monks',
they carry their found deer legs to the barnyard,
hungry as they are with the old longings for flesh
we had thought they had lost and forgotten for good.

The youngest dog comes leaping for the house,
his front legs tucked tight against his chest,
his hind ones stretched out in a fair and fluid
imitation of the deer he has helped to gnaw
toward the bone-hungry, frozen ground

Two mongrels give up their playing with a bone
that's not much good for anything but play
this time around and lies finally abandoned
on the field like a dropped baton. The brown
hair, soft as a girl's, fringes the fibula.

I wonder what sounds the hunters have left
in the woods next to ours, what echoes of old
cheers have hollowed the trees, how much
deer mew we will find in the spring suspended
there above the dog yap and the shouted guns.

Coming to Ground

Not fully rooted from the ground, too early turned
to penmanship and numbers, the boy had climbed at six
from boredom, from the fear of being schooled
by taught men. Those things he was at five, the feel

of tree toad, the easy chemistry of rocks, the sway
and swing beyond geometry, they would have him name.
One day, then, finding a familiar tree, he climbed
away from what they knew, clawed old ways up from danger.

A tail twitch startled in some sleeping cells. His lips
relearned the snarl, his throat the guttural.
He climbed, climbed, would not come down to ground
though those who named him numbered in their anger cries.

His favorite football player came, uniformly stuffed
with autographs, with kid gloves on. The round priest,
full of the sins of childhood, came to bless him down.
Beneath the tree, the fire engines fought for space,

raising arms to have first crack at him. And overhead,
the helicopter hovered, heeled, puttered about in pauses.
His mother cried and cried. Beyond assurances, he sat.
Beyond pterodactyl, brontosaurus. Eventually, he slept.

In dull of dark, with all the namers gone, he woke
to shapes that shaped him as he stared. Common-sensed then,
he downclimbed woods that had been only sure before,
coming at last to ground in the uncertain world of men.

C&O Tow Path

A skunk painted the edge of the canal
ahead of where I walked. Its lines
defined what was and was not mine.
The dark heaves of it fell off the white
and blended with the shadow where it sat.
Such subterfuge was little use in Washington,
I thought. The shadows changed. The dark
gave way to light. The grave, still savor
of the skunk broke all to bits and what
had seemed a skunk, delicate and debonair,
shrunk to life as a sullen plastic sack.
But farther on, there, there at the river's bend,
something is stirring in the underbrush.
Something worth the walk, still as it is.

Cocktail Loungers

At the bar are seven barflies,
balanced on their stools,
antenna raised in hope of prey.
Life equals art.
They look like fighter planes at rest.

Also at the bar are butterflies
with long breasts twisted into yesses
and other birds, unwinged,
who twitter, momentarily,
of spring.

At tables all around are sitting citizens
at play. Like toads in bogs, they bulge,
mouths open should a bird or bug
come near. Art equals life.
Picassoesque grotesques, they bulge.

Doorman

For Tara

The night we heard the news from space,
my daughter, who is three, remarks
with no surprise but careful to instruct:
"The moon is like a doorknob,"
to that other self all children seem
to have and have to answer to.

I sit trying to construct a poem of praise.
Spacemen and women stumble down the page.
She says again, impatient to be gone,
"The moon's a doorknob," and,
already dressed to play outside,
waits for me to open up the sky.

Geometers

Boys on skateboards gaining ground, go off
the solid pavements we have built for them.
Flat-out, they throw what's only theirs to throw.
They arc what matters of the curves that we
have graphed to show that fun is mathematical.

The ride is sickle-taught simplicity,
uses gravity to groove the air
to one matched pair of hemispheres,
as if to dare euclidean geometers
to demonstrate more pure parabola.

They know we mean no harm who keep our feet.
On the air they write their hieroglyphs,
substantial as our axioms,
to be deciphered by the non-substantial boys
who will follow them into the solid air.

Now they show us how to go.
Their young boy arms arc us out from charts
toward some new geometry. Forever pushed,
they lift our noses off the stones, our ears
from off the dully beating ground.

They teach us how to listen to the sound
of formulas they write on stairs
unproved, unprovable, immaculate, of air.

Hack

Spring is a shack with the "s" unhinged
by sunschemes. Spring is something to get
into so you can drive around the blooming park.
Spring is a hack, the merest bud of the hackles
that will be raised by summer's holy heat.
Spring is hackleberries that aren't finished yet.
It's the hitch of the slipping trousers
of a man the cityslickers would call a hick.

Spring is a hillybilly's "Ah, what the hack,"
as he throws off the dead weight of Appalachian
winters, chokes his cold to an early grave,
gets in the car and drives, lickspittle quick,
to meet the girl in the hack in the park
whose name, the girl's, is April May,
whose smile unshackles his locked heart,
loosens his tongue, puts him in happy hock.

Just for the heck of it, he cocks his head,
chews a couple a dozen peppermint chiclets,
prepares to kiss that April May to a swoon
like they do in the movies, shivering shucks.

Sunday at Seven

For Brenna

"Popeye," she says, or sometimes "Lassie's on."
The darkness flattens out, retreats.
Ribbons of Lassie run across a dozen lawns.
She, a stern-faced seven, settles in her seat.
One Lassie settles down to do good deeds.
You, in a hurry of Sunday, mix the salad. I,
pale caveman, fix the fire
to keep the wolves of night at bay, the sticks
brought wholesale from the lumber yard.
Our strange magician daughter, discontent
with good dogs saving sheep and doing tricks
now sits, transfixed, intent on terror,
while through her all-electric home
a minute werewolf stalks minutely screaming maids.
But she's at home with terror, with a yawn
she points, young sorceress, her magic stick,
shuts off the sound. The fire sputters, dies.
Wet green woods, I mutter, while she flies
into the kitchen shouting, "Dinner's on."
And who am I to doubt that fires fly
through green woods in the certain dark
of dawn? And who to doubt that darkness dies,
that wolves retreat before a stern-faced seven?

Pig

"All over Europe the people believe that
one's fate is tied up with its afterbirth."
Standard Dictionary of Folklore

Because, in the dim forest where I was made,
my mother, out of shame and patience

with my wrinkled face and the bloody mess
that followed my birth, threw out as worthless

that which did not belong to her,
because a rooting hog ate the shadow of what I was,

as if it were his to start with and end,
I will gorge myself, anchored deep in mud,

I will fatten myself like a fool to be fed
to whatever hungers hunger to be fueled.

My hair will grow in tufts from corrugated warts,
my eyes will shrink to black pennies, swart

skin will circle my vitals, I will not see the wind.
I will deny myself nothing I can reach, define

what I am with great roiling grunts, with oily squeals.
Only at night, in the dark that writhes like eels

will wings push out like flowers from my sides,
will this mud be a path through the beaconing sky.

Baltimore Stoops

In Baltimore the women stoop
still at marble steps and scrub
what is theirs of glory. The steps
give passage to everything they face.

They dress a street that's dirty and cracked
as the ocean gets before a storm.
The women on their stoops lean up
the tilting street to talk or have a sip

of tea. One's had a husband leave her
once a year for over twenty years.
One will die of what she doesn't know
she lacks. Their narrow houses, rowed,

bear them along what's shoaled, what's
deepening. They show their entrances, white
as pearl, pearl-veined with the graying
delicate lines of lives unconquered and marine.

Trying to Get to Brooklyn

That lady in the feathered hat and pink brassiere
yoo-hooing taxi-cabs in downtown New York City,
that lady used to be the citrus queen.
Coiffed and chaperoned extensively,
by camera, comb and boy cajoled,
she rode the finest float in Tennessee
down through Florida to the sea.
Now she clerks at Macy's, selling cold
Long Island women Clairol's lemon rinse.
Now, five falls away from innocence,
she stands still in her pink brassiere,
too young to smile, too old to wince.
The cabbies, heading west don't even leer.

Fourth of July at the VFW

At a point of land that pencils out
Into the bay, the local VFW guards
the old guys from their wives,
lets them pretend toward
some foreign shores again.

They throw a party for the Fourth
and everybody comes: pampered babies,
oldest men in rubber pants,
women whose teeth chatter all
about their Yankee Doodle Dandy.

Small boys ready their oh's
like cannon. Their mothers block
the babies' ears with thumbs as thick
as muffins. The rockets promise
much, rising on white chargers.

What happens then is nothing
much, nothing but the dried out
dribble of a slack mouth falls
from a height where was meant
to blossom flowers of pyrotechnic

and lilac suns and, for the vets,
a field of fifty stars sewn in a sky
of red and white triumphant over seas.
The crowd stirs its last eyes
into the dark and hearing only ffffft

Turn to their empty cars, their sights
Fixed on a better time than this.
Above them, the moon bucks and rears
in its traces, throwing the ocean around.
Stars that went out before we began

steer them on their way. A comet
sharpens itself along the dark.
Seahawks hit the black water and come
Up silver, slashing into the void
Between the rising fields, going home.

Charles Atlas

You who are pressed tuxedo-tight
in preparation for the feast
pantomime before the bedroom glass,
masking what you will become.

First you're Charles Atlas, rescued from
the spineless backs of comic books.
As he returns your stare, slack muscles
harden, hearten what you are.

But then another window shows
another panel from the comic book.
The skinny little kid you like to kick
kicks your heart with the car he's got

and blonde blonde blonde who helps him drive
away from your window, out of sight.
You flex a flinch at your mirrored life,
stern and relieved. You put your face

against your face and change the toad
to Superman. Prepared at last, you retreat
and pirouette down basement stairs
to hot dogs, television, quarts of beer.

Autistic Child

He sits in the puddle of himself,
splashing water on his chest and arms.
We have no record that he has ever sung.
We have no record that he has ever talked,
save for several sounds he makes
that none of us can understand.

His face is a corkscrew, twisted
Into wine beyond our telling.
His face works and the pavement streams.
Ribbons of the world bear him away.
This afternoon, late, he will return
to rest on the banks of himself.

In that light, his face will grow
to a silver drop. His voice, that none
of us can understand, will write his name
on the ground. His waters run
from creek to river, ocean to sky.
Fruit and flower follow from his cries.

Proverbial Man

"Every animal is sad after intercourse"
—Latin Proverb

Ah, that Roman, making proverbs after love
in the late olive afternoon, making the next
generation of proverb-makers. What did he see
in the still eyes of the woman
that he cried after?

Those animals he knew most were himself
and stray cats that he kicked down Roman alleys
when no one looked. And once a lioness
that he saw, in heat, who tried to love
the man she had just mauled.

What did he see in those still eyes?
His own going out? Rome burning through desire?
The stray cats breeding tigers in his blood?
His own sperm burning toward the fatal egg?
The slave rose up to swallow Africa?

Tamed on this long chain, we make love
to ourselves and after, laugh at proverbs.
We know those animals who once were sad are dead.
Beyond all pain, our laughter leaks into the night.
Our leashed cats wait, watching with still eyes.

Rural Free Delivery

What weighs heavy, like a letter postage due,
is a certain silence, not of your own choosing, not
like a letter you've sent but one you haven't gotten.
All over Rural Free Delivery 1 and 2
people wait for answers mailed under cover
to questions asked so long ago they are forgotten
or didn't matter anyway. What has come
in time is the new *Saturday Evening Post*,
what has come is the new *Life*, promised once
a month, as glossy as the old one ever was,
and a gross of bills shouting for payment.
What has arrived in briefs, is yesterday,
what we bought then, thought then, broke then:
slicing machines, old poems, Federal codes.
The man who was going to write hasn't.
The woman who thought she had, hadn't.
What falls from envelopes unarrived in waiting rooms
is something as heavy and as soft as summer squash
thickening in the unpicked garden, yellow, silent.

Letter from the Hunger Artist

Dear Edgar Allan,
        As you will have observed,
they stagger along their own flat feet,
rise each time as if for the first time,
flap around like a boy's toy of a bird.
Stiff and useless as crutches in water,
their used-up legs trail out behind them.

Earlier today, a gang of them scraped
at my door, eating the Halloween corn
as if their dark hearts had never heard
the farmer's gun. Their beaks on my lintel
rapped like rats' feet, like bone.
On Wilhelmeminstrasse, as you already know,

a congregation of them has settled down
like silence, like blackened clots
from a hemorrhaged grove of elm like one
you used to love. They slump toward
each other, wings broken to the ground.
Only their eyes are busy.

As you may guess by this letter, I have gained
a crow myself. This afternoon, flawed by sundrop,
as if on signal, there has come a bird to roost
would put your raven's "nevermore" to shame. He has
with single purpose broken through the bay window.
The shattering glass rings still with light applause.

I end in haste. Blood follows after him.
You will find us practicing our changes.
I am teaching him how to walk like a citizen.
You would like the ways we have come to terms,
the appetites I am learning, have forgotten.
Yours in hunger from the other side,
                        Kafka.

Dopplegangers

At weddings and funerals you see
them more and more, the ceremony
of the world becoming one.
A man you've never met walks past,
trailing behind him a family
as familiar as your own, the hawk-
nosed aunt in the shapeless print,
a boy who could be you splintered
to her hand. The stranger's wife
could be your mother, years ago.
His mother, bringing up the rear,
reminds him of the food you have
to pick up at the grocery store.

You will learn to recognize, admit,
the fingerprints whose marks are found
on bible and gun as yours although
you will swear you've not been near
the place before. And you'll be taken
for another with a smile you will learn
to like before it goes away, comes back
for good, leaving its teeth behind.
The babies that you did not have
will look, someone will say, like you.
You will laugh at that, remembering
your uncle's face one day before you knew
the ceremony of the world becoming one.

Rounding Things Out

One day, when he lathers up his face
To shave, he feels the nipples tighten up,
his chest buttons down to stop the swell.
Next morning his stomach roils, throws him
up the stairs in a hurry. He gags, his mouth
a gargle of woolen socks. He wonders what
is going on inside.   His appetites exhaust him.
He takes and takes. Women he doesn't know
have things to say to him, call him "Honey,"
help him in and out of cars. His belly swells.
He thinks its cancer, hides it from his friends
by blaming it on beer.
He wears a face he hardly recognizes, his mouth
serene and settled above the secret growth.
He gets preoccupied with calendars, counts
ahead and behind on fingers, toes, gives up
his season tickets, sickens, takes to bed, to pain.
The head comes first. He thinks of round
as yellow. electric, sharp as ice.
The shoulders ease out next, then an elbow, knee.
The sac is slipped. He lies back, spent,
knowing he will never be the same again,
counting the seconds that fall between breaths.
wondering who he, was before this all began,
how his blood could only circle like a business man
taking the train to work and back from work.

Lost Ark Animals

In the moonlit loss of earliest morning
they come from the sea, two by two,
pulling with them the legs they have lost
or never found, shouldering up the beach
away from the sea's demands.

We have names for them that we cannot
remember or are forbidden to say aloud.
You will know the ones we mean.
Something in us has called them out.
The messages they bring are those of the other,

the shudder and slap of the broken boat,
a whistle pitched through the melted wing,
a willing gene of the chromosome pinched
in its rush by it own blind needs.
When the sun has come to be what we know

as sun, they will go from us as from anything
that is less than loss. They will snuffle
themselves inside a curl of the turning sea,
as flat and white as the two blank eyes
of something fully gone, something that we mean.

Phillips Gallery

Morris Graves is gone,
has been removed from the darkened room
and packed away until a simpler time return
when men can spend their nightmares in the gallery.
In his place, the colors of hysteria.
His forms too angry for before, his colors, gray
and black, too measured out of pain for now.
Variations on a canvas cut from life,
cool moods of almost and after all,
cool glimpses into worlds of night
he wrought.
Sandpiper, snail, and snake-winged bat he shaped
(or hinted that he shaped,
sometimes the signature was all).
If love-leaked, light comes new into our rooms,
we will uncrate fierce Graves and hang him up
again to watch night wake upon the wall.

Japanese Writing Box

Even the reek and wrecks of last night,
steeped beneath the willow trees
that line the streets of Shinjuku,
have order to them, will disappear
as the day quickens onto Tokyo.

The early morning band of boys,
uniformly bound for school, tend
the corner of the morning they own.
Only their faces bloom above the black
and polished suits that sheathe them.

An old woman, as bent and defiant
as the cypress tree, grows yellow flowers
from her knuckles. We would like to see
her eyes which only care to see the street.
We might as well ask a ginko to speak to us.

Nothing is ever finished here in Tokyo,
nothing reaches beyond the crane's flight,
the crane's shadow. The ravens will come
to the willow trees and find the seeds
and sun beneath the wrecks and reek.

The boys will board the bus
and make a science out of going on.
The old woman will straighten out
at the sound of the plum bud opening
to the rising sun, hearing the poem

she has left across the pavement.
Her smile, which we will not understand,
will mark the day and place for us in ways
we will not remember, can not forget.

While we watch, a language past
another rendering writes itself down
in a careful antique shop, the owner
guiding the delicate strokes, the blunt
lines that picture themselves. His pen

drawn from a crane's wing feathers, dips
into an ancient oriental writing box
that knows the way to capture candle black
until the water finds its way to ink.
The writer brushes what was only smoke

and water onto paper rolled from rice, a kind,
he says, that can absorb the textures of Japan:
an old, woven face, the ravens' coats
of luminous blacks, the schoolboys in
their autumn grace and light solemnity.

Coffin Bone

Horses carry coffin bones around against the unlucky break,
just in case the body needs one to keep things clean,
to get a step or two on the field. The thoroughbreds,
they know a little lead at the top of the stretch
means an extra bag of oats, warm hands on the hocks,
soft words from the hard man they know as Luke. As luck
decides inside the hoof, the bone will open like a gate,
the angles polished by sure hands, the break as truea
as the racing surface isn't. The funny bone is the last
to know, cracks up as funny bones will at the sharp point
that being made about rounding onto what can not
be ignored. The funny bone and the coffin bone,
old buddies, together through mostly thin, the first
and last to get the joke, to have the largest laugh.
Luke will miss them. They know how to finish fast.

Sunbathing

These morning gulls mean business, fly
like thrown knives, looking for something to stab.
Later in the sunfed day, they will be content
to pose for pictures, come down to bags of boys,
crack up the sky and us with their antic swoops.

Now they are what keep the small fish small.
From sixty feet they drop to eat, white shields
that give pause to the sea and to us who watch.
The gulled fish, borne at last to air,
learn too late that there are things to fear

more than shark, still water, and the lures of men.
Inland they fly, cradled in the cropping beaks
that show them what will not become.
I angelwing in the wand, wash in the sun,
pretending such flights are done for man.

Sound Levels

The 747 tunnels overhead, breaks
the day to pieces in this little town
that's buttoned down between two fields
and quiet as the past on postcards.

The mockingbird knows other sounds.
Its calls have reason on their side,
and hunger, and knit the sky together
that has been torn by what is above.

And what is below, the eyeless mole
that feeds on bugs from sunken trees,
hears things I could not think to name,
hears nothing of the business overhead.

A glove of night cups me. I am still
in sleep, dreaming the sound of clematis
climbing, finding ways to get around
without the ears I could not do without.

Prostitute in the Cancer Ward

She will bloom soon.

For twenty years her hips helped
men disconnect themselves from sons
they could not bear, from daughters
rich and fertile as the black earth
that the men had grown to fear.

She stuttered out to say her piece
to slot-faced customers, their eyes
slit down to facets of themselves.
Gauging costs, they talk her down
to give themselves a double pleasure.

Now, her belly sags like a bag of waters,
droops toward the hard Nevada ground.
The cells collect a thing no man can buy
or sell, a thing that will lift and open her.
Full of what she has become, she flowers.

Aioi Bridge, Hiroshima, 1984

Tiresias, disguised this time around
as an old Japanese stone mason,
offers me a piece of what had been
Hiroshima, a hunk of wall that could
Have come from Thebes, it is so cold.

As big as a loaf of unleavened bread,
Another age's building block, this stone
 is blessed in being here at all,
half of it blackened with the August rain
that rose from the ground like the dead.

The mason, his voice as high and hard
to read as birds', gives me a place
between the rivers to carry out
what can be found of the ancient city
fallen down and risen now around us.

I take away what was not built to stand
alone. I take it though I should think
to test the truth of the black rain
by biting down, or else I do bite down,
as metalmongers have taught me, and find out.

I take it though I think I've read that with
the night my tongue and gums will bleed
unstoppered through my broken, blackened teeth,
my chromosomes will wrinkle up with loss,
my eyes burn in a vast, unequal sun.

Afterwards, I scrub my hands for days
or else I don't. I forget even if I go
shamefaced to our customs clerk,
confess I have no rights to what I have.
I remember only the old mason's face,

the way it carves a language out of sounds
my ears can see, the words are that bright,
the way that antique incantations work
like hands on building blocks he has found
to give away from what we have lost.

Chicken Piecer

The knife hand opening the jugular
like a letter, the practiced skinning out,
The quartering to marketable size and taste,
of wishboned breast, of wing, of thigh,
The calculated piecing finally gets her down.

She makes amends. Her house collects in praise
Of cocks and hens. She drags the straw for eggs,
For soft bones, pores through catalogues.
Porcelain Rhode Island Reds, crowing clocks,
Whatever takes a chickens shape, she buys.

She warns her husband far away from all
Her chicken things, tells him to keep his thumbs
In his palms, his various machines (hammer
And wrench, irons and putter, electric drill)
Away from what is hers. She makes a blanket , one

To dress her bed, a full-pieced quilt, patched
With fretted coops and scarlet wattles. She works
The colors into place the way she has seen
The sun do, sliding gradually past the gray roost
Of the morning, filling in the piecework day.

She needles as she goes. Her fingers fly
Like cutter and cut, defining her design.

Highway Man

I harvest failure all along this road while crows
circle and dip, fluttering black wailers, cawing woe.

This mornings haul is harrowing.
These broken bodies, pheasant, skunk, sparrow,

need mending more than I have time to spare.
I gather rags and tags of bone, frozen stares

of disbelief. Sometimes I think the two night eyes
of trucks, impossibly wide, hypnotizing,

while thirty tons of metal hurtle onto two
pounds, more or less, of life. For the few,

this roads a nightmare dying. Cars, morning-sighted,
steer around the bodies. The drivers' eyes look right,

getting to work. My work's the waking of the dead.
My truck, their funeral bier, blinks a requiem.

I gather heaps of skin and rags of broken bones.
Apart from men, I mourn this morning's haul alone

Autumn Moon Garden

My neighbors world is World War II.
Twice he has told me that his father died
a Kamikaze, altering the old Pacific's face
a dimpled moment, freckling it with boys
from New York State and then himself.
I've met him in the darkened street to hear
him say his oldest boy committed Harakiri
at a college somewhere in the west.

We walk his garden, named the Autumn Moon,
that draws the suns that fall ahead and fall behind.
He shows me how his bonsai paint the foreign air.
Their peerless branches feather out a separate peace.
He points out Hirohito, late the Emporer,
trooping from every knob, from every gnarl.

Ludwig van Beethoven: Notes on a Testament

Ludwig van Beethoven, that pockmarked, ugly man
who walked along with his stubby fingers clasped
as if to hide behind his back,
who had a notable for making enemies,
one day wrote a testament:

> *You fellow men*
> *who believe or say I am ill-bred*
> *and your enemy, you wrong me with others.*

This testament he wrote to his brothers
with the instructions: "To be read
and carried out after my death."

> *You do not know*
> *the secret reason for what is mere appearance.*

Named Ludwig for a brother dead in infancy,
those secret mother-griefs breasted with mother's milk
to Ludwig living, he grew in his own secret youth
a growth of spongy bone enough for twenty ears, not two,

a bony field which blocked his brain
from the slight delights of shepherds' flutes,
the hoarse cacophonies of fishwives everywhere,
the quiet tones of friends, lovers' whispers.
One day this proud man wrote:

> *It is almost two years*
> *since I have given up the company of other people*

To his friend Franz Wegeler, he wrote,

> *because I cannot say*
> *to them I cannot hear.*

Ludwig van Beethoven, dubbed The Rude, who in his pain
wrote only what he heard as hearing died
and all that pain turned on itself, who one day
in his pride and prime, to the poet Goethe,
walking side by side, to gentle Goethe
twenty years his senior, shouted ironically
(about the bowing folk who passed them by,)

> *In your humility,*
> *Your Excellency should not worry,*
> *Those bows, perhaps, are only aimed at me.*

This ill tempered boor from Bonn, this hunched-in man
sure only of his inner ear, his pain-taught harmony
wrote anyway those pieces he called the Fidelio,
the Missa Solemnis, and thirty two sonatas for piano.
From memory and those secret reasons clutched inside
(his teeth tight-clenched to the acoustic stick
pressed as he composed, to the piano),
he wrote those symphonies which leak
the secret reasons into our humble, gossips' ears
waking us to sounds beyond appearances.
His testament, those secret sounds of every day
which now, a little more amazed from year to year,
we play and play and play.

GALLERY III

Landscapes

Industry, 29" x 22", watercolor

Autumn, 36" x 22", oil on canvas

Setting Sun II, 20" x 20", oil on panel

Cloud Red, 55" x 28", oil on canvas

Anna's River, 31" x 47", acrylic on canvas

Winter, 31" x 37", acrylic on canvas

from ***Making Beds***
1989

Mary Cassatt

You know how some parties are not parties
at all, how she will have to sit in a boat
for hours, overdressed, a baby in her lap,
a small smile you have learned can taste
like poison on her lips.

You are aware of the shoreline he approaches
blind, his back turned at the oars' command.
You see the steep city that teeters on rock
and, to the left, the road that empties on the sky.

You would like to believe that it is Sunday,
that the sky and the water are as blue as paint,
that she, with her only family, is on a boating party.

Over his shoulder, though, you let her see what is coming.
You slash her red mouth shut, let her say nothing at all.

Making Beds

For Brenna and Taea

I take my daughter to the county dump,
show her how to get rid of things,
a lesson in learning what to keep.
We drop off what we've brought to sink
into this place, an iron bedstead
bent beyond repair, some boxsprings

corkscrewed past belief, the flotsam of
the life we've made. It scares her so
at first she starts, this stink of twists
and turns, the crux of melted junk
and beauty burning in a turned-up field.
The buzzards in their rags become the field.

The bulldozer snorts and bellows in its heat,
as brightly yellow as a Christmas toy.
I show her the detritus of our common lives,
the spiralled rust of boys' tossed parts,
dead dolls, the delicate skeleton of a cat,
the plastic spoor of the comfortably fed.

She wants no part of what we have to share
of loss. She shows me how a throw of gulls
lifts and settles like a muslin sheet. She says
the gulls and buzzards mind their place.
She knows of other things she's made to do.
She's learning how, she says, to make her bed.

John Sloan *The Ferry's Wake*

Approach John Sloan,
a man who in such a sea
is little more than shadow,
less substantial than you
are used to on this run.

Though he looks at the wake
as if he means to jump,
though he seems to be part
of the darkening sky,
though he stands too close

to the black accordian gate
that's there to stop a child
from finding out too soon
what it means to be
in the ferry's wake,

though he paints alone in the stern
unfriendly light and will not
probably be pleased at the pause
you offer, approach. He will tell you
stories of the harbor, of the winter

afternoons he has made of this,
this passage that you make now
together, of how, one time, a small
dog leaped, snarling at the wake
as if he saw a threat, a ghost

in the foaming black. Greys, John Sloan
will point out for you, can make
for seeing things that aren't there,
greys and the sea and the lowering light
that comprehend the crossing sky.

Blueberry Woman

The blueberry woman has wrecked her week
and the kitchen, baking muffins, baking pies.
She reeks of blueberry jam, has steeped herself
with thoughts of blood and bloody butcherings.
What she comes to at the end, and prints
in blue juice on the bathroom door,
is the family's menu for the harvest month.

Her children, home for lunch and stuffed
with chalk, a permanent peanut tbutter glaze
to their eyes, are served up to their regret
grilled blueberries au gratin, blueberry soup,
blueberry tart in blueberry juice, then spooned
out the door and back to school, their faces
drained, their mouths as dyed as grief.

Her husband attaches his way from work, dulled
to boldness by drinks with the boys. What he
expects for dinner is baked potatoes,
New York Strip, asparagus with hollandaise.
He also expects the kids to be fed and bathed
and ready for bed and his wife dressed up
for dessert and ready, by god, to roll. She is.

She darkens up what is dull about the meal.
What he gets is blueberries a la carte.
Blueberry hash he gets and blueberry toast
and blueberry sauce for the blueberry mousse.
As he nods off in bed she leaves him lack
and blue. Dressed to kill, she heads outside.
A blue moon ripens in the letting sky.

In that new light, she murders what
she can, the strawberry beds,
the blueberry patch, rows and rows
of tomatoes. Come the next harvest,
her family can eat flowers, as far as she's
concerned. Roots they can eat, or seeds,
rainbows, daffodils, stripes of the blue moon.

Crossing at Lumberville

There are several ways of getting off
this bridge and boys of an uncertain age have tried
them all. The Delaware beneath is swift but sure
of its own depth, runs easily, has gathered up
the downhill drift of water from the Catskills through
the Poconos and its conniving streams and spread
to touch and separate two otherwise united states.

The bridge walks its way from Lumberville to Raven Rock.
Halfway across, a line is drawn that jumping boys
must pass. It's forty feet above the river's run
and in the air beyond the latticed rail where they hang on,
talking things over as boys boys will do, deciding
if and how such crossing can be made.
The few who've gone ahead are resident below.

They mock the bridgelocked with easy voices, newly deep.
They own whatever bank they've drifted to and are as sure
of foot as they will ever be, borne beyond by walking,
briefly, on the air. Above, the boys who count have
indecision on their side, more sure of growing up
for being less. There will be time to jump at Lumberville,
they seem to know. That's why the bridge is here.

The ones who turn away suppose that any way they go
will have its own demands. They talk each other toward
whatever's to be crossed right now. By summer's end
they each will make the leap and walk on water for
a twinkling, then sink in a spell to the river's bed
and rise to float, seabound, downstream.

Marking the Orchard

Old Lucas Marvel totes his urine out
to the apple orchard every night last thing
before he goes to bed. He circles the trees,
spells out their names in Palmer Method
strokes and swirls to pass the time
and keep the orchard free from deer.
His spinster sister Hilda has her way
of marking too. She stops at Henry Cronin's
Barbering Shop on Saturdays to gather up
the random hair of men she might have known,
waits until her brother locks himself
inside the crazy quilt, his long form scissored
out in sleep, then makes for the apple orchard
with her apron full. Skirts hitched, she
sprinkles the gathered hair on the ready ground,
naming to herself her names. Jonathan and Baldwin,
Ben Davis and McIntosh ripen with such maiden care,
such husbandry, safe from the burning eyes of deer,
the lifted heads, the shining, blunted teeth.

Clam Shucker

Her gnarled knuckles figure out her age.
She has worked many things, has sewn the breasts
of turkeys back together each November
of almost sixty years, has broken necks
of chickens when she's had to, and for the life
of her, she's shucked an ocean full of clams.

The cold of a hundred fathoms works into her bones
like sly eels. Sometimes the rust of sunken ships
comes drifting to the tips of her fingers, then
she flexes them like puppets, making songs
to match the waking shapes. Sailors, brown
and full of spice, walk the line toward her.

At times her hand sits, a foreign country
that has occupied her, a brazen toad squat
and lewd in her green lap. But then the shapes
come slipping in between the swollen cracks
like treasure undersea, like dead men
rising with the tide. Those songs are hers

that give the frozen knuckles hope to add,
such songs that swelling burst and break
her fingers loose, that send the writhing eels
wrinkling back to sea, that mend the shells
and broken wings flapping in her fluid bones

Country Play

The toy gun loads itself into his mouth.
He squeezes the day from his eyes.
What's left is an empty circle of sun,
Paling like the early moon he saw
The night his father bled the pig.
These contradictions always make him sad,
Though not enough to cry, enough to swell
Inside him like his mother did that time
In pictures that he keeps upstairs.
The background for his play is corn,
the green ears breaking like culs de sac
from the straight and narrow stalks,
and beans climbing like marines
up the perilous lattice strung between
two crutches left from when he broke
his foot, his only break before or since.
He has told the neighbor girl what he's
to do, has satisfied the cat, left cryptic notes,
and stands now in the heady sun of afternoon
his left hand pressed against his ear to kill
the sound. His trigger finger fondling the future
jerks and jerks again, practicing what's fatal
in this country scene, for later.

GALLERY IV

Portraits

Naya, 16" x 11", oil on canvas

Behind the Scene, 36" x 24", oil on canvas

Grigorski, 18" x 12", oil on panel

Museless, 29" x 22", watercolor on paper

Table for One, 28" x 20", oil on canvas

New Old Hat, 22" x 18", oil on canvas

Winter Song, 11" x 22", oil on panel

Self Portrait Under the Weather, 36" x 24", acrylic on canvas

Prince Richard, 22" x 16", oil on canvas

from ***Appetites***
2000

Appetites

Because yesterday I ate shark steak,
the thunder walks for hours on the house,
the boneless hips of giant fish snake
toward the town. Because the filets, scored
from the dorsal side, wavered in the frying pan
like flung birds, the Bradford Pear bows down
to its knobbed knees to give full lift and sway
to wingless things whose silhouettes darken
the stark sky under which I have to navigate.
Because the meat of the shark tasted as clean
as chicken would if chickens had the chance
to eat the sea, the black in this place swallows
the light that I have made to hide myself away.
Tomorrow, because the shark has lost all of his skin
and his only blood vein, I must offer my legs
to the sea, up to my belly in fingers and feathers
of surf. I have other mouths to feed because
yesterday I ate a sound I never had the chance
to hear, nor wanted to, nor knew I did, till now.

Eating Around the Gizzards

Not even sick, I fall to chicken soup
in the kitchen where I sometimes live.
The broth is thick with cures.
C's of corpuscular celery,
noodles meant to strengthen breath,
Odd bits of chicken check everything
from rickets to sclerosis.

I eat it all, spoon it in like penicillin,
castor oil, Carter's Little Liver Pills,
all into my mouth and down the gullet
like heaven's medicine, all except
the gizzards that lump the bottom
of the dish like sunken lungs
or fallen angels' wings.

These I eat around and around
until they are alone, staring up
from the slicked bowl as sad
and reproachful as old diseases
I think I am well rid of,
I am sure I have never had.

Troubles

Troubles locked in memory
a trouble told is a trouble lost
the trouble with troubles
medical troubles, marital troubles, martial troubles
the trouble with luke and amy
the troubles of the world, the troubles of the word
a trouble found is a trouble gained
a trifle of a trouble doubled twice becomes treble trouble squared
that's troubling you is troubling me is troubling us
troubles mumble
eat a trouble for indigestion, teach a trouble how to skate
trouble is the mind's rubble; trouble is the mind's measure
trouble is mind, saith the mind, trouble is mine
troubles dealt with in the morning makes the evening wet
child trouble, parent trouble, in-law trouble, outlaw trouble
troubles break
troubles bake until they burn
troubles turn and bite the hand that breeds them
troubles learn to hide in unswept corners
troubles forgotten
trouble said tongue-tripping fast becomes a babble
troubles blown up become a bunch of smithereens
trouble trouble boil and bubble

Breaking Fast on Sunday

The hunched man at the counter,
has finished all of the scrambled eggs
and soft scrapple he can eat in faith
on a Sunday morning after church.

He says as if to himself but loud enough,
just loud enough for the couple who
glaze over in the booth behind him to hear,
for the woman in the other booth

who fans out like a bat at her food,
for us, fed full and on our way to someplace
else that what he needs from them, from us
if we wouldn't mind, are our bones.

For his dog, he says, for the pup who waits
at the window of his car, and knows the bones
are inside. For myself, he says to himself,
to the greased year, I wouldn't ask. The hound

though, he has learned to wait like waiting itself.
Come Sunday, something to go with church,
and the family car and the family drive,
come Sunday, he has to have his bones.

We don't answer him, not one of us,
not being, as it were, directly asked.
We take our bones out to our own cars
and drive away with everything we have.

On the scrambled table one of us leaves toast,
a trick he has learned, a way to hide the tip.

Turkey Buzzards

There's a story that the old guys tell
to us new guys in Southern Delaware
about a thin canal got dug by hand
a hundred years ago. The labor came
down Delaware Bay then overland, men
a year away from farms they couldn't keep
in Ireland and Italy, what our own farm boys
called them Far-and-nears.
Or, if that was beyond them, Joes.

What really got the present old guys,
makes the whole thing worth telling, is the part
that makes them cackle like some hens that need
to lay an egg. Those Joes, can you believe it,
would sneak up on a swoop of turkey buzzards
who were sneaking up themselves
on something else to make sure what was lying down
had nothing left to worry on. And then those Joes
would jump a buzzard and knock it silly, all at once.

And what do you think those Joes did then? Et it.
Yessiree, right there. Et that buzzard down
and went on back and dug some more canal.
They'd shake their heads, the old guys,
eyeing us to see if we believed it,
hearing it again. Et those turkey buzzards same
as you or me would eat a rabbit, eat some chicken.

Honey Man

The honey man licks himself
clean for the sweet taste of bees,
for the texture of honey on skin,
for the heavy murmur of the hive.
He won't have honey in the house
for his children's sake.
He knows the hungers it will bring.
He has watched the sweet stick of it
seep through glass, through skin.
He will not make his daughters live
as he, wash their hands till they bleed,
scrub the whisper of hives from their ears.
Himself he scrubs again and again.
The thought of honey, the sweet prison
it makes of his fingers, he has confessed
to the priest. The bees tumble their hungers
around in his brain. The bees in their pinafores,
in their union suits, the bees
in their private, impeccable hive,
The motors of the bees
hum him awake and to sleep. And he,
for his children's sake, circles the house
he has made, erasing the smears of sweet
and the ways to the rooms of the honeycomb.

Gallery at the Tate

Edvard Munch's *Sick Child* 1907

Such scenes are posed, of course,
The twenty-eight children perched
On campstools in front of Munch's
Fire, the teacher tribing them
About the sick child Munch has caught
Who must herself one time have posed
At being well but now is stuck for good
In bed, a study drawn from life.

Munch has got it right, they see.
The lie of being young and sick at once,
The lie of being made to stay in bed
Is something that they know as well
As their skin, a lucid parchment the girl
Who lies before them cannot mend or hide.

That Munch pretends to keep her alive
Is something that hurts them to attention.
She has their sympathy, but chooses rather
To look away, over her mother's shoulder,
Beyond her mother's bowed head. She does
Not want to see the way her mother's hand
Has reddened with a mother's shame

Exactly to the shade of her child's hair,
To the rusted color of blood. She does
Not want to see the children unfold their
Legs to follow their teacher, to find
Their beds, to find the studios and sick
Rooms that will make them real and her.

Freshman Year

Wednesday mornings, after Mass,
the giggle of the sophomore girls hot
as purgatory on our freshman ears,
we'd leg it up the hill away from all
that heat toward the certainties of first
year science, Algebra, *amo, amas, amat.*

Our school was just a mile from the valley
school where the girls pretended they
would all be nuns. We learned our lessons
there, some of them, high on the coal
slag side of Manayunk, twenty minutes west
of Philadelphia's City Hall and Billy Penn,

his iron eye, his Quaker hat, his history.
We chased our breaths up the winter hill,
heartsick only for the cream-filled doughnuts
waiting with our Gallic Wars for us to mouth
with hungers old as battlefields each time.

I have eaten nothing since as rich
with sin denied as those baked bribes
of Brother Hausfeld, who also showed
us how to mend equations, how to find
the area of a trapezoid and, later,

how to die. The girls are gray now, fat
with grandkids and the century. But that
was 1950 and the war was over years ago,
and the Philly hills that didn't all run up, ran down.
And all that winter long, the snow gave like sugar
doughnuts, topping our hunger, hiding our tracks.

Steak and Kidney Pie

I order up a steak and kidney pie,
Being in London and required,
but have to turn it away for fear
the kidney will stick to mine,
make me more of a pisser than
I already am. It's always the way.
I eat a cottage pie, I start to grow
thatch and thistle, walls all around.
I drink a whiskey. I want to sweep
the whole place clean. The ways
that I become the things I name,
I better stay away from Bartlett Pears
or I'll double up the problems I are.

Bonesman

Giacometti cuts
through the fat,
a butcher bound
for bone, gaunts
us for widow's soup.

Giacometti's knife
stalks the streets
of Paris, points
him and us toward
the vanishing line

we walk.
The bones of
Giacometti's
needling eye
sharpen

what is lost,
punctuate
a century
we leave
behind.

Grieving, for Five Voices

I want to get his ass cremated
quick, get the ashes back, spread
them in the driveway, run over
the son of a bitch every day.

The first six months, Friday nights,
I'd set the wash machine on heavy load
and talk myself through a couple cycles,
talk it silly, talk until I'd spun dry.

Same as always, I make the drinks at six,
Vodka Gimlets on the rocks. We work
things out as the dinner cooks.
I finish mine, toss his in the sink.

Didn't anyone tell me how to spell it out,
what I'm supposed to do I'm lucky enough
the bastard dies before me, didn't a one
give me the book on what to do about it.

Every night, I take off all my clothes
and climb into his pj's, bottoms
first. It's like entering a flower
and wrapping it around me, close.

Omnivore

When I was ten, my father was a cannibal.
In a single month, I heard him order liver,
spareribs, brains, and kidney stew.

I almost gagged. Like Hannibal
I crossed an Alp to get away from him.
My equipage was vegetable. I foraged fruits.

I never passed his way again. I ran faster
than the bulls and never hurt a one.
I refereed two wars in hideless boots.

I found out what was really what on Sanibel,
an island tight with Florida. A girl I liked
more than my Quaker Oats said I had no roots

worth cultivating, that she had had enough
of my braggadocio, how I ate oranges as if
they were lemons, that I was food for fools,

not her. These days, I eat what's on my plate
to expiate the lean forbearing sins of sons.
I brother all who practice bellylaughs.

GALLERY V

Abstracts

Abstract Forest, 27" x 31", acrylic on panel

Blu Comet, 35" x 28", acrylic on canvas

Color Fantasy 2, 20" x 28", ink and acrylic on paper

Cosmic Silence, 23" x 39", watercolor and acrylic on canvas

Terrain I, 22" x 29", ink and watercolor on paper

Cosmic Fantasy, 30" x 22", watercolor on paper

Cosmic Blue, 22" x 30", acrylic and ink on paper

Earth Orange, 28" x 20", acrylic on canvas

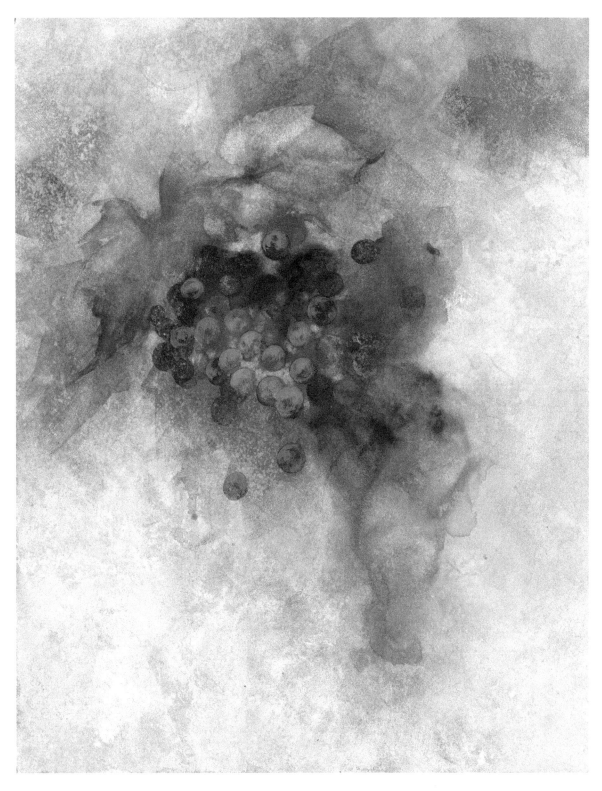

Grapes, 29" x 22", watercolor

Migration, 45" x 90", acrylic on canvas

Cosmic Explosion, 20" x 40", acrylic on canvas

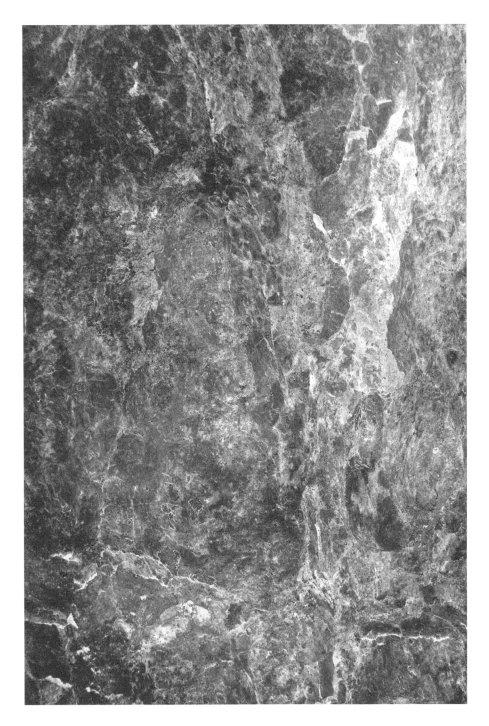

Terrain II, 22" x 29", ink and watercolor on paper

from ***Circling Out***
2007

Loaves and Fishes

For Theresa

Five fishes lay like loaves of bread
Unleavened, waiting for the oven.
You, like a lover, gentle them into place.
They have come here by a long way.
Their bellies have scraped seastone
Older than the loam of our fathers' farms.
Their flat eyes wear a world that is now
Too new to comprehend. Secrets they have
Are nestled down in corners of a hill
Two hundred fathoms low. So they have come
To die, taking everything they are and were
Out of the hooked world that teased and caught
Their hunger like a skulking thief.

You, who have not killed anything
Except perhaps some drying parts
Of yourself, feed their dead, dread bodies.
You balm them with a lemon's blood.
On the parchment brown and winter ground,
Small birds bury and unbury spring.
Their sickled beaks break the cold's codes.
You, the birds and the fish liven what starts
At stone. We, who do not remember what
You cannot forget, require a lesser loam
To grow what's winter in us. In a fish,
You find and feed us spring. The birds
And you remember what it is to dig.

Universal Donor

Today, I gave away my liver, heart, and lungs.
My daughter starts it. She tells me it's a way
Her friends have of beating radar traps,
Staying in the fast lane as long as they want

Actually, my purpled aunt, she starts it.
She gives everything away that can be used
When she is maybe seventy and gone South.
About a decade later, on a trip back home

And thinking maybe she is going to die,
She calls around the local undertakers',
Hoping she can rent a casket, get her body back

To where she has made the promise. Her God
Is a traffic cop. She gets off with a warning,
Lives another ten years, sleeps her way to an easy death.

What I'm wondering, how it's going to feel
To have my heart inside somebody's chest,
Thrumming out my rhythms when I'm dead
Like some jazzman on Bourbon Street.

Guess I'll let the deal stand. The odds are good
At least I'll either beat a speeding ticket
Or live a little longer than the rest of me.

The odds are better the rest of my life
I'll feel like a music man with golden shoes,
Walking around with money to share
And nothing to spend but a little time.

Safety Pins

Holding things together.
Gravity does that—and rainbows
And the man who figured out
That gravity needs rainbows
As much as the other way around.
Safety pins do that—if you happen
To have your trousers falling down
Around you, if you happen to be
A baby in the days before Velcro.

Mothers too. They're safety pins,
The lot of them, holding things together
That otherwise would fly apart,
Putting back in shape the ripped and torn.
Bracelets too, the way they hold the wrist
At Peace, the way they add a little grace
To the hand's need to give and take.

You find a bracelet made of safety pins,
Dressed in rainbow, bound by gravity,
You've got a thing worth hold on to,
An ornament to hold the day in place.

Water and Words

with thanks to Emily Dickinson

The only thing my mother feared of death
was the pain she wasn't sure
a woman her age should have to take
who was too old in her stooping years
to be afraid of God, needles, enemas,
or children's nagging tongues.

We tried to mother her the way grown sons
think they have the right, the supporting arm
around the folded wings, the voice straight
out of Jimmy Stewart or Henry Fonda.
I'd never use that voice with my own kids,
they'd laugh me out of the neighborhood.

I know enough I'd never try such guddle
with my history classes of oldfaced high-
schoolers chewing on the lessons of the past
with certain smirks before they rested their fore-
heads on the kidneyed desks they'd about outgrown.
But with a mother I never understood would die

I used forgive me life the sickly touch of sons
when all she wanted was a cool glass of spring
water to wash away the fog in her throat,
water that had been someplace holy, that
and a couple answers to a crossword puzzle,
just a couple hints so she could finish off
the Sunday Times for once, for good and all,
and guess that it and all things else were right.

My Brother's Whistle

Frostbitten mornings, waking up
I'd hear him whistling home from the paper route.
"Off We Go Into The Wild Blue Yonder"
and I'd be in a B-52 inside a nest of fighters,
And Yankee Doodle laughing his way
From the halls of Montezuma to the shores
Of Tripoli and once in a while a doleful Irish tune
about young boys dying for Mother McCree.

I'd hear him from the top of the street
the clip of his step, the lilt of the pitch,
pinch my lips together and blow—hard—
my tongue fluttering like a lamed sparrow.
Nothing happened except one day he ripped
his cheek on a broken bottle of soda
and I worried he'd never whistle again.

            I spent the next couple of years
learning in high places how to catch a note
in my mouth and push it gently with another
and another until I had it right. By then,
he'd stopped whistling and discovered girls
Who didn't care what tunes a boy could carry

First Catechism

For Shannon Elizabeth of the Rivers

So now you're here and the world
is a wobble better than it was before
and promises a deeper travel
into space than we can guess.

Such rare turns move us
toward a distant star, a dot
as luminous in the night sky
as an island's winking beacon.

So welcome, slight child of rivers
and mountains, welcome to those
you hadn't met till a day ago
but have changed as surely and ever

as wheel and tool and word.
No going back on it now, Babe.
Hit the afterburners. Let her rip.
You may cry as if you don't know

the way but we know you do and we
intend to follow where you flow,
the way oceans turn on their heels
at the moon's command. Before

you forget: Does the moon cry?
Can the sun run? What does the rain eat?
Will willows ever laugh? How goes gravity?
Where will you not be, now that you're here?

Tackling Time

Under the circled print of the crucified Christ
we played tackle football on our knees
and prayed when we had to that the mother
wouldn't call us from our game. As a penance.
For the sacrilege. For being boys in a time
of war. And the bloody Jesus above the mantle
judged every play. The rules were plain enough.
One against two each time. Crawling runner rugflat
for the three count. Piling-on allowed. Four downs.
His glassed-in eyes followed us from rug end
to chair leg and back again. Kept score. Knew
the clock was ticking but never said a word.

We didn't know enough to read the Ref's eyes
and stop before it was too late. No happy storms
all winter unless the Christ came down, unlocked
His arms, our hearts, the sleds in the cellarway.
Good snows, we'd hitch rides on nervous cars,
get towed for blocks. We knew that wouldn't happen
now, anymore than the war would end tomorrow.

Those eyes. Above the kitchen table, FDR hung
smiling until the mother let us know about the food,
how cold it was getting. How we'd clean our plates
if we had to sit all night. She told us enough the father
heard and sent his voice ahead of him down the stairs.
Nothing though could shake us from the game until
the radiator rattled twice about the cellar's dark,
about the ashes that wanted lift and drag to the street,
the bushel basket lighter for the fire, and rattled again
as God's bones didn't have to. And too, the stare.

Freight Yard at Night

A railroad cat I knew a while ago, slung
belly emptied out of kits, took the night I met
her to show me and them the how and what
of finding food through our own resources
for when she was gone or worn down.

She'd drag a mouse center-stage, give it
the old Ouija eye designed to mesmerize,
leap and cuff in one fluid motion, just enough
to stun the smell awake so she could carry one
of her kits over to nose the proper food for later

when she was too cat-happy lazy to feed the no-
good nearly-growns. The railroad that hired
college kids to fill the jobs of the crew clerks
and freight car checkers on vacation
hired me because my father worked in

that same freight yard for twenty years.
He knew how to get me on the third shift.
The job taught me about late nights,
the taste of three o'clock heavy as lead
on the tongue, the jilly-joy of going out

to count the coal cars newly arrived,
the way dark sounds were always ahead
on the tracks, knocking on the grimeglazed
windows, making things that shouldn't do so
creak. I'd pretend the only good guys left

were me and the crew clerk for the main line
against the gangs of thugs and mugs
coming down the tracks on either side.
We spent the summer like quicksilver, we
and that railroad cat who had her litter right

before the tom cat arrived and ate three of them.
I didn't have a girl to tell things to, what I'd seen,
so I went out and got one, the standard issue
smart-between-the-ears kind, the way girls get
way before guys do from our quaint bringing up.

Later

For Davis Galvin

He would like to know when he gets to touch
the paintings, when he gets to rub his wet nose
on the belly of Aphrodite, when he is allowed
to sing in the confessional. He would like to know
when they will stop putting signs around the property:
No Hunting, No Talking
No Making Hay or Babies Without Permission.

He needs to know why none of the signs
Say please. Please make a U-turn Here
Please do not drive 92 miles per Hour
Take Your Time, Please, to Enjoy the Do
Not Enter Sign before You Don't .

He would very much like to talk
with his mouth full and chew
with his mouth open. Sometime
soon he would like to go where
he shouldn't and do what he can't:
ride a skateboard up the isle of St. Peter and Paul's,
example one, while the Pontiff is pontificating
or ride the same skateboard, example two,
through the cosmetics section of Saks Fifth
Avenue, dribbling a basketball and a cherry popsicle
Down and out in a stream of red and flash.

He would like to know when he gets to stroke the sad-
ness from the Mona Lisa's eyes, when he gets to climb
the trees and monuments and the Empire State building
when he gets to go deeper into the forest,
hide, with the giraffes, behind the giant stones.
He would like to know when we get to the part about the girls.

Introductions

I remember the miniature and plastic saints when
I was a kid better than the names of soldiers I met
in the maybe war and I remember those men better than
my children's friends and I remember those lads
better than the man I talked to last week on the telephone
who may buy five thousand pair of the underwear I have
to sell to meet my quota for the month. Or else.

And I have to meet that man tonight, among people
that I do know and do remember and he doesn't
and I have to introduce him as if I knew his name
as well as I know my brother's, who I sometimes
can hardly remember at all anymore, he having left home with
all the toys and half our parents' lives before I had a chance
to tell him goodbye and went off and didn't remember one night
(so I have heard, so the story goes, so I tell my kids)
to put his flak jacket on before he went out to take a piss
and instead took a bullet through his stomach that took
one week's worth of pain to realize he was never going to digest
and died and I remember better even than my children's names
the day we got his mess kit back from the US ARMY, courtesy
of the RED CROSS, and inside it was tucked this three
inch plastic Blessed Virgin Mary, the same one that one of us,
I can't remember which, got as a prize for selling the most
punch-out card chances for some gigantic gift that I forget
but probably had to do with a Chocolate Easter Bunny
stuffed with jelly beans or a subscription to Boy's Life,
or The Messenger of the Sacred Heart.
So tonight, when it's all on the line, when I am about
to be hung out to dry like those 5000 jockey shorts I will
never sell after this insult, I'll lean back on the air
as if my brother were there holding me up, I'll reach
inside my watch pocket of the vest I only wear
when it's all on the line and fondle for luck the 3 inch
plastic BVM that I have kept for more years
than I can remember and then I will remember
the fool's name just like that. Or else, like that, I won't.

Gazetteer: A Map of the Known World

For Brenna & Chris

The way to what you want is through the door.
Follow the turning moon to where it lies.
I cannot tell you less or lead you more.

Remember what you knew when you were four
and all the locks were set against your size.
The way to what you want is through that door.

Put on the heart's disguises. Go. Explore
the space you have to fill to recognize.
I cannot tell you less or lead you more.

You will find the bridges out, the road detours,
Polaris lost in cloud. The usual signs.
The way to what you want is through the door.

Atlantis underneath will wave. Before
You're there, you'll look Cyclops in the eye.
I cannot tell you less or lead you more.

The magnetic compass only fixes north
in shaky place. Like us, you walk wide skies.
The way to what you want is through the door.
I cannot tell you less or lead you more.

Geography Lesson

Practice mouthing syllables just after the announcer.
Learn to spell from the headlines.
Speak the text as you read until your tongue curls up.
Roll the names out and away from you like tank treads,
clear and unambiguous and foreign:
Cechnya, Al-Khader, Khasavyurt, Pyongyang.

It must have been this way in County Cork
for the Irish girls mastering the American,
that wondrous sound that swallowed up their uncles.
The girls would do the words to each other
the way the nuns had taught them how
to do the decades of the joyful mysteries.
Fingering the beads, they'd recite the names
enough until they wouldn't stumble once:
Appomattox, Antietam, Chickamauga, Manassas.

The thing that's good about this easy way
toward a knowledge of the world and all its places
is the certain promise of a new list coming soon,
strange sounds that come off the lips like prayer.

Toad in the Garden

I started up a toad as I dug out
a weedbreak so the daisies and roses
could have a chance in this rapacious world,
A toad the size of an infant's thumb, maybe the first
of his time to be startled into memory this spring.

He squat-jumped toward the neutral ground
Welcoming little but hunger, the way teen-agers do,
keeping his unblinking eyes on me, who must
have seemed a monster mouth and on his turf.
And then, like tightly funneled sand, he began

his backing into the camouflaging dirt,
slowly, ever so slowly, taking
his haunches underground while those eyes,
wise as survival, kept track of hungers he
might have guessed were bigger than his.

He wriggled until the darkness took him in
and though my earthbent stare tried hard to hold him,
he became in a wink a hint of browner dirt.
As I watched he left me there alone,
and let me know a secret for my eyes:

how they are allowed to see a little bit,
then nothing much, then everything at once.

Circling Out

From Nadolony she came, Mary Lenio,
To a tiny town in Pennsylvania, a place
stuck like a fist into a mountain of coal.
As if she were part of the creation myth,
she found on that mountain a man
Whose name she had known in her village
An ocean away. What she found with him
Were children she had hidden under her eyes,
Braided into her hair, secreted beneath her skin.
The way things come together and circle out,
Others came to touch her world. She opened it
And took them in. Husbands for her girls,
A wife for the son. They came from Finland
To find her, from Mayo and Dublin and Cork,
From Brooklyn they came, and Columbus, Ohio.

One Saturday night, among the kielbasi, perogi,
Galompki, she found a dozen grandchildren
With more pouring in the windows and out
From under the beds, playing hide and seek
Among the cabbages and apple trees, churning
Their joy, leaving lip prints all over the house.
She has gathered them all into her apron,
Shaken them out like seeds, sprinkling
The country around. The fields of her flower,
Spreading color through the gray evening,
Calling birds we've only heard in dreams.
They will go out, those fields, those blooms,
Those fluting birds, will circle out endlessly,
From the sure center she was and will be.

INDEX of TITLES

Acknowledgments

Grateful acknowledgement is made to the editors of the following journals in which these poems first appeared:

Antietam Review: "Greening the Ford"; *Argestes*: "After the Battle at Seven Pines," "Saying Goodbye," " The Big Leagues"; *Atlantic Monthly*: "Passive Aggressive"; *Best American Poetry, 1997*: "Introductions"; *Big City Lit*: "First Catechism," "Enough"; *Blue Unicorn*: "Autistic Child"; *Bogg*: "Grieving for Five Voices," "Coblentz's Farm"; *Broadkill River Review*:"Goat Farming At Flat Rock," "The Season After and Just Before," "Play Things," "Blind Girl," "The Egg Man in Warsaw," "Harley"; *Chachalanan Review*: "Gazetteer"; *Cicada*: "Aioi Bridge Hiroshima, 1984," "A Clean Well Lighted Place," "A Sensible Sleep In Time of War"; *Common Ground*: "Aioi Bridge Hiroshima, 1984"; *Commonweal*: "Informal Fallacy," "Eating Around the Gizzards," "Still Life Study," "Heron Bay," "Leaf Raker"; *Country Mouse*: "Baloney Sandwiches"; *Delmarva Quarterly*: "Artisan," "Beyond the Hot Sun," "Corn Silk," "Weekday Morning," "Catching the Waves"; *Descant*: "Rape," "Crossing at Lumberville," "Learning to Forgive"; *Dogwood*: "Sounds of an Afternoon"; *Dryad*: "Sunday at Seven"; *Feila-Fiesta*: "Antietam's Bloody Lane"; *Four Quarters*: "Freshman Year"; *Frigg: A Magazine of Fiction and Poetry*: "Old Photographs," "Summer Spikes," "Second Light at the Uffizi"; *Poetry*: "Immigrant"; *G. W. Review*: "The Burgers of Calais"; *Image*: "Tackling Time"; *Innisfree Poetry Journal*: "A Closer Look: Martin Galvin, 22 Poems"; *Isotope*: "The Scientist's Prayer"; *Journal of the American Medical Association: JAMA*: "Surgeon's Appetite"; *King's English*: "Gravities"; *Milkweed Editions: Salt Marsh Anthology*: "Heron Bay"; *Mona Lisa Anthology*: "Later"; *National Honors Report*: "Blueberry Woman"; *New Republic*: "Apprentice Chef"; *New Verse News*: "Advice To War Poets"; *NW Zoo Review*: "Black-Eyed Boy"; *Notre Dame Review*: "Later"; *Ohio Journal*: "Clam Shucker," "Marking the Orchard"; *Perigree-Arts Magazine*: "Finding Loss in a Flemish School"; *Poet & Critic*: "Sex and the Single Rover," "The Toad In The Garden," "March 3, 1998," "Office Visit"; *Poet Lore*: "Fingering: A Way to Count," "Hilda & Me & Hazel," "Birthday Poem for Lizzie Borden," "Country Play"; *Poetry*: "Universal Donor," "Water and Words," Marathoner," "Widower at Work"; *Poetry East*: "Safety Pins," "Thoroughbred"; *Potomac Review*: "Tackling Time," "At Their Math," "Geography Lesson"; *Science 84*: "Doorman"; *Sows Ear Poetry Review*: "Cream"; *Spirit*: "Phillips Gallery"; *Texas Review*: "Making Beds"; *Unicorn*: "Baltimore Stoops"; *Vulgata*: "Weathering the Front Door"; *Washingtonian*: "C&O Tow Path"; *Washington Review*: "Charles Atlas"; *Wind*: "Small Town Satyr"; *X: A Journal of the Arts*: "Loaves and Fishes"; *Zone*: "Ox-Eye Daisies."

A note from the poet's wife:

Special thanks go to Rod Jellema, friend and fellow poet, who never gave up on helping us get this book out. He spent many a Saturday or Sunday afternoon over lunch visiting the inexplicable possibilities, or lack of, in the where and the what and the who of the poetry world. Marty and Rod also spent countless hours mulling over the hundreds of poems Martin has written in making selections for this book. It was Rod who sent us to a wonderful publisher, Richard Harteis, who took great interest from the start in publishing the poems of this deserving poet.

So, too, goes a very special thank you to Richard Harteis, Director of the William Meredith Poetry Foundation, and his press, Poets Choice. His enthusiasm, praise for, and excitement about publishing this book has been boundless since the start. His support, guidance, and patience throughout the entire process of pulling a book together for publication has made it easier than it might have been. Thank you, Richard Harteis, for your encouragement and faith in moving this project along. Your persistence and dogged tenacity has made this book happen.

–Theresa Galvin

And a note from the poet:

A special thank you is due to Terry for her attention to many details of publishing, hours upon hours she might have spent on her painting.

Self-portrait with Raven

About the Artist

2000–	working independently in Hamburg, Germany
1995–2000	working independently in Amsterdam, Netherlands
1993–1995	Florence Academy of Art, Florence Italy
1990–1993	Pennsylvania School of Art and Design, private study in Atelier Richard House
1985–1989	BA, English and Philosophy, College of William And Mary in Williamsburg, Virginia

See ryanbongers.com for additional information

Artist's Statement

A word about painting

I feel empowered wielding a brush. My head and my hands are happiest dipping in to get dirty. With color, I stake my claim and howl my decree. Moving paint is an act of invention and discovery, a means of diving into ethereal then surfacing into real. A source of inspiration and affirmation, the medium provides me with a vast and open arena to capture and convey.

Some thinking, little planning

There are two of me at work in the studio: one is deliberate, contemplative, the other rash and restless. I rarely make preliminary drawings, but react instead to visual clues—a whiff of something real, but veiled, which I attempt to explore and expose on canvas. The process is mostly intuitive, involving much trial and more error.

Plunging straight into color may be haphazard, a reckless use of time and material, but I enjoy the immediacy and suspense of working at full throttle, allowing the stuff to surprise me.

I use oil for portraits and pieces requiring more precision or polish, and acrylic or water-based mediums for abstracts and bolder statements. Oil paintings are forged in the classical fashion, upright, at the easel, while the acrylics remain flat on the table or floor, to allow the saturated colors to flow.

A day's work

So what exactly have I achieved after shaping a head into a portrait, or squeezing a still life from a bunch of lemons? Do my emotions dictate which colors to use, or do the colors drive my emotions? The act of using a brush loaded with wet material to bring an imagined thing to life remains elusive, if not downright shifty. And the performance can be both meditative and manic, demanding guts—like all creative endeavors—and a great deal of honest reflection and introspection, plus a cool capacity to eliminate non-essentials.

Is any of it meaningful, or even relevant?

I don't know. I just paint.

–Ryan Bongers

A Note About the Author

Award winning poet Martin Galvin has been writing poetry for more than 60 years. Having spent his working life teaching at the college and high school level as well as at the well-known Writer's Center in Bethesda, MD, he managed to produce five books of poetry and hundreds of collected and uncollected poems over the years.

Martin Galvin's first book, *Wild Card,* won the 1989 award of The Poetry Committee of the Greater Washington, DC Area, published by the *Washington Writer's Publishing House*, judged by Poet Laureate of the US, Howard Nemerov. Galvin's poems have bccn published in numerous journals and magazines including the *Atlantic Monthly*, the *New Republic, Best American Poetry 1997, Poetry* and many others. Several of his poems were awarded first prize in national contests: "Freight Yard At Night," *Potomac Review*, 1999 (Jane Shore, judge); "Cream," *Sow's Ear Poetry Journal*, 2007 (Linda Pastan, judge); and "Hilda, and Hazel, and Me," *Poet Lore,* 1991 (Thomas Lynch). He was awarded a residency in 2007 for artists at the prestigious Yaddo, the 400 acre estate in NY founded by wealthy New Yorker Katrina Trask in 1929. He was also awarded Summer Fellowships from the National Endowment for the Humanities at Stanford University (1984) and Columbia Univesity (1993).

Galvin has been honored by the community he has lived in for over 50 years, Montgomery County, MD. After teaching at St. Joseph's College in Emmitsburg, MD for 5+ years, he moved to Chevy Chase where he taught at Walt Whitman HS, and The Writer's Center where his students were mostly working professionals. He received the 1989 Maryland "Teacher of the Year Award" and a "Master Teacher" award where he exchanged places for a year with a University of Maryland teacher in the Honors Program in an interdisciplinary program, taking classes with his UMd students in such varied courses as Geology to facilitate this approach. He was recognized by the Universities of Chicago and Rochester and by Williams College with an "Excellence in Teaching Award," nominated by his former high school students. His poems were selected several times to be displayed in the Poetry Gallery at the Executive Mansion, Rockville, MD; he received the Montgomery County Arts and Humanities Award in 2001. The Montgmery County Public Arts Trust selected his poem "Doorman" to be featured on one of the Bethesda 8 Trolley Poetry Benches in downtown Bethesda during its recent redevelopment.

Martin and his wife, Theresa, have two daughters Brenna (CA) and Tara (PA), two sons-in-law, Chris Sidhall and Greg Curry, and four terrific grandchildren: Sarah, Shannon, James and Davis.

This new collection, *A Way To Home: New and Selected Poems*, comprises some of Galvin's newer poems (since the 2000's) and many selected from his other five books.

Martin and Theresa Galvin can be reached at the following: galvinte@yahoo.com or galvinhimself@yahoo.com